The Soup Cookbook

Recipes for Soups, Stews, and Bowls for everyday home cooking.
100 Easy and Delicious Homemade Meals.

William Lawrence

Leave a review about our book:

As an independent author with a small marketing budget, reviews are my livelihood on this platform. If you enjoyed this book, I'd really appreciate it, if you left your honest feedback. You can do so by clicking review button.

I love hearing my readers and I personally read every single review!

Dedication

This Book is dedicated to my mentor and my true inspiration - my mother. All my childhood, I grew up watching her cook delicious delights in the kitchen using home-grown organic produce, and that made me fond of eating healthily and cooking quality food, all while creating new recipes.

Table of Contents

Introduction 7

Spring Soups 9

Summer Soups 33

Fall Soups 57

Winter Soups 81

Stew Recipes 105

Bowls Recipes 129

Conclusion 140

Introduction

What is Soups?

Soup is the perfect cozy meal for any time of the year. From traditional vegetable soups, such as minestrone, to unique speciality recipes like Thai coconut lemongrass, a steaming bowl of soup has the power to nourish your body and soul. Soups are versatile enough to be served as starters, main courses, and even breakfast dishes for those cold winter mornings. With just a few simple ingredients (stock, vegetables and proteins) you can whip up a delicious meal full of flavor in minutes - which makes it one of the easiest dishes to make without sacrificing quality. No matter if you're looking for something quick and convenient or something that will feed a crowd with minimal effort, soup is always an excellent choice.

Soups come in all different shapes, sizes, and flavors, but what exactly makes something soup? The answer may surprise you. Soups can be anything from a delicate vegetable broth to hearty bean chili. They can contain noodles, potatoes, vegetables, beans, and even meat. All that is needed is some sort of liquid base. Broth, stock, and cream are all popular bases for soups. In other words, anything that you decide to put into a bowl with a liquid and heat up until it's cooked through can be considered soup! So, get creative with your next meal and try something new - it may just turn out to be AMAZING soup!

Types of Soups

Nothing compares to a hot bowl of soup when you're feeling under the weather! A nice, steaming-hot cup of broth can make all your worries seem infinitely better. And with such a wide selection of soups out there, there's something for everyone! From classic French onion soup to creamy potato bisque and traditional chicken noodle, the possibilities are virtually endless. Or if you want something truly unique, why not try some yummy pozole or Udon? Variety spices up any meal and helps keep it exciting – so why not give one (or more!) of these delicious soups a try? Not only are they sure to please all palates on a cold winter day, but they're also easy to prepare in a pinch!

Importance of soups

Soup is an important part of many diets, as it is typically nutrient-dense, low-fat and filling. It serves as a great source of nutrients such as vitamins, minerals, proteins and carbohydrates. The water content in soup can help to keep the body hydrated, while its fiber-rich ingredients aid the digestive system. Soups are also often easy to customize according to individual tastes and preferences. Adding different vegetables or proteins can easily enhance the nutritional value of soup dishes. Finally, soups are convenient meals for individuals who have limited time for cooking and preparing meals, since many are relatively quickly to make and come in a variety of flavors.

1. Soups are a great source of vitamins and minerals. They can be made with a variety of ingredients such as vegetables, meats, beans, and grains that provide essential nutrients. For example, lentil soup is rich in iron, potassium, magnesium, and zinc, while chicken noodle soup provides protein, B vitamins, and other minerals.
2. Soups are an excellent way to use up leftover ingredients. Whether it's cooked meats and vegetables or scraps used for broth, soups make it easy to turn them into a nutritious meal quickly and easily.
3. Soups are typically low in fat and can often be made without added oil or butter which makes them an ideal choice for those watching their fat intake.
4. The liquid content of soups can help to keep you hydrated throughout the day as well as provide warmth during colder weather months. Soups are also easy to digest since they are already broken down from cooking which makes it easier for your body to absorb nutrients from the ingredients used in the soup itself.
5. Finally, soups are incredibly versatile; there is a wide variety of recipes available from all corners of the world that can provide different flavors, textures and experiences depending on what type of soup you make or buy. From light broths to thick stews - there's something for everyone when it comes to soup!

You will find lovedly recipes for every season!

Spring Soups

Classic Chilled Almond Soup

Preparation time: 15 minutes
Total time: 15 minutes
Servings: 6

Nutritional Values:

Calories 223, Total Fat 16.6g g, Saturated Fat 1.8 g, Cholesterol 0 mg, Sodium 79 mg, Total Carbs 17.8 g, Fiber 3.3 g, Sugar 9 g, Protein 4.2 g

Ingredients

- 1 cup blanched almonds, soaked overnight in water and drained
- 2 stale white bread slices, cut into cubes
- 1 apple, peeled, cored, and chopped
- 1 small garlic clove, peeled
- 1 cup cold water
- 1-2 teaspoons sherry vinegar
- Salt, as required
- ¼ cup olive oil
- 1 cup seedless green grapes, halved

How to Prepare

1. Place the stale bread in a high-powered blender, add almonds, bread cubes, apple, garlic, water, vinegar, and salt. Pulse until smooth.
2. While the motor is running, slowly add in the olive oil and pulse until smooth.
3. Transfer the almond soup mixture into a serving bowl and place in the refrigerator to chill before serving.
4. Just before serving, top the soup with grapes and serve.

Classic Carrot & Ginger Soup

Preparation time: 15 minutes
Cooking time: 35 minutes
Total time: 50 minutes
Servings: 4

Nutritional Values:

Calories 121, Total Fat 4.4 g, Saturated Fat 3.2 g,
Cholesterol 0 mg, Sodium 503 mg, Total Carbs 17.2 g,
Fiber 3.8 g, Sugar 7.1g, Protein 4.1 g

Ingredients

- 1 tablespoon coconut oil
- 1 medium brown onion, peeled and chopped
- 2 garlic cloves, peeled and minced
- 1 long red chili, chopped
- 1 (1/3-inch) piece fresh turmeric, peeled and sliced
- 1 (¾-inch) piece fresh galangal, peeled and sliced
- 1 (¾-inch) piece fresh ginger, peeled and sliced
- 4 cups carrots, peeled and chopped
- 2 lemongrass stalks
- 2 cups water
- 2 cups vegetable broth
- Salt and ground black pepper, as required
- 2 tablespoons fresh cilantro, chopped

How to Prepare

1. In a large-sized-sized soup pan, melt coconut oil over medium heat and sauté onions for about 5 minutes.
2. Add in garlic, red chili, turmeric, galangal, and ginger. Sauté for about 5 minutes.
3. Add carrots, lemongrass stalks, water, broth, salt, and black pepper. Cook until boiling.
4. Adjust the heat to low and simmer for about 15-20 minutes.
5. Remove the pan of soup from heat and discard the lemongrass stalks.
6. With a hand blender, blend the soup until smooth.
7. Serve immediately with the garnishing of cilantro.

Classic Split Pea Soup

Preparation time: 15 minutes
Cooking time: 45 minutes
Total time: 1 hour
Servings: 6

Nutritional Values:

*Calories 441, Total Fat 16.7 g, Saturated Fat 4.9 g,
Cholesterol 30 mg, Sodium 1401 mg, Total Carbs 44.6 g,
Fiber 17.7 g, Sugar 7.7 g, Protein 29.5 g*

Ingredients

- 1 tablespoon extra-virgin olive oil
- 1 cup carrot, peeled and chopped
- 1 cup onion, peeled and chopped
- 2 garlic cloves, peeled and minced
- 2 cups dry split peas, rinsed
- 1 teaspoon dried rosemary, crushed
- 1 bay leaf
- Salt, as required
- 6 cups vegetable broth
- 6 cooked bacon slices

How to Prepare

1. In a large-sized pan, heat the oil over medium heat and sauté the carrots, onions, and garlic for about 4-5 minutes.
2. Stir in the remaining ingredients and bring it to a boil.
3. Adjust the heat to low and simmer, partially covered, for about 30 minutes.
4. Discard bay leaf and remove from the heat.
5. Set aside to cool slightly.
6. In a blender, add the soup in 2 batches and pulse until smooth.
7. Return the soup into the same pan over medium heat and cook for about 4-5 minutes.
8. Serve hot with the topping of bacon slices.

Classic Bacon & Potato Soup

Preparation time: 15 minutes
Cooking time: 40 minutes
Total time: 55 minutes
Servings: 6

Nutritional Values:

*Calories 291, Total Fat 17.5 g, Saturated Fat 6.5 g,
Cholesterol 40 mg, Sodium 1198 mg, Total Carbs 18.1 g,
Fiber 2.9 g, Sugar 2.4 g, Protein 15.6 g*

Ingredients

- 6 bacon slices
- 1½ teaspoon olive oil
- ½ cup celery, trimmed and chopped
- ½ carrot, peeled and chopped
- ½ onion, peeled and chopped
- 4 cups potatoes, peeled and cubed
- 4 cups chicken broth
- Salt and ground black pepper, as required
- ½ cup cheddar cheese, shredded

How to Prepare

1. Heat a large-sized-sized soup pan over medium-high heat and cook the bacon for about 8-10 minutes or until crisp.
2. With a slotted spoon, transfer the bacon onto a paper towel-lined plate to drain.
3. Crumble the bacon.
4. In the same soup pan, heat oil over medium heat and sauté the celery, carrots, and onions over medium heat for about 4-5 minutes.
5. Add the potatoes, broth, salt, and black pepper. Bring to a full rolling boil.
6. Adjust the heat to low and simmer for about 15 minutes.
7. Add in the cheese and stir until melted completely.
8. Serve immediately with the topping of cooked bacon.

Creamy Garlic Soup

Preparation time: 15 minutes
Cooking time: 1 hour 10 minutes
Total time: 1 hour 25 minutes
Servings: 4

Nutritional Values:

Calories 341, Total Fat 23.4 g, Saturated Fat 12.5 g,
Cholesterol 62 mg, Sodium 142 mg, Total Carbs 17.1 g,
Fiber 2 g, Sugar 3.8 g, Protein 1.9 g

Ingredients

Roasted Garlic
- 2 garlic heads
- 1 tablespoon olive oil

Soup
- 2 tablespoons butter
- 2¼ cups white onions, peeled and sliced
- 1½ teaspoons fresh thyme, chopped
- 18 garlic cloves, peeled
- 3½ cups vegetable broth
- ½ cup whipping cream
- ½ cup Parmesan cheese, finely grated
- 2 tablespoons fresh lemon juice

How to Prepare

1. For roasted garlic: preheat your oven to 400 °F.
2. With a small-sized knife, remove the top of both garlic heads.
3. Lightly brush the garlic heads evenly with oil.
4. Sprinkle them with salt and pepper.
5. In a piece of heavy-duty foil, wrap the garlic heads.
6. Place the foil packet of garlic onto a rimmed cookie sheet.
7. Bake for approximately 32-35 minutes
8. Remove the cookie sheet of wrapped garlic heads from oven and place on the counter.
9. Unwrap the garlic heads and set them aside to cool.
10. Squeeze the garlic heads into a glass bowl. Set aside.
11. Melt butter in heavy-bottomed large-sized saucepan over medium-high heat and cook the onions and thyme for about 6 minutes.
12. Add roasted garlic and raw garlic cloves and cook for about 3 minutes.
13. Add in broth and cook, covered, for about 20 minutes.
14. Remove the soup pan from heat and, with an immersion blender, puree the soup.
15. Return the soup pan over medium heat.
16. Add in cream, salt, and pepper. Bring to a low boil.
17. Drizzle with lemon juice and serve.

Creamy Green Pea Soup

Preparation time: 15 minutes
Cooking time: 20 minutes
Total time: 35 minutes
Servings: 4

Nutritional Values:

Calories 150, Total Fat 5.2 g, Saturated Fat 2.7 g,
Cholesterol 14 mg, Sodium 621 mg, Total Carbs 16.6 g,
Fiber 5.5 g, Sugar 6.2 g, Protein 9.5 g

Ingredients

- 3 cups vegetable broth
- 3 garlic cloves, peeled and minced
- 2 tablespoons fresh mint leaves, chopped
- 1 teaspoon curry powder
- 14 ounces frozen green peas
- 1/3 cup heavy whipping cream
- Salt and ground black pepper, as required

How to Prepare

1. In a large-sized-sized soup pan, add broth over high heat and bring to a full rolling boil.
2. Add garlic, mint, and curry paste. Stir to combine.
3. Adjust the heat to medium-low and simmer, covered, for about 5 minutes.
4. Stir in the peas and simmer for about 5 minutes.
5. Remove the soup pan from heat and set aside to cool slightly.
6. In a blender, add soup in 2 batches and pulse until smooth.
7. Transfer the soup into the same soup pan over medium heat.
8. Stir in cream, salt, and black pepper. Cook for about 3-5 minutes.

Cheesy Bacon Soup

Preparation time: 15 minutes
Cooking time: 30 minutes
Total time: 45 minutes
Servings: 8

Nutritional Values:

*Calories 570, Total Fat 47.7 g, Saturated Fat 22.8 g,
Cholesterol 136 mg, Sodium 1711 mg, Total Carbs 3.3 g,
Fiber 0.7 g, Sugar 1.2 g, Protein 32 g*

Ingredients

- 1 pound bacon, chopped
- 2 celery stalks, trimmed and chopped
- ½ of medium yellow onion, peeled and chopped
- 2 cups chicken broth
- 1 tablespoon minced garlic
- 1 tablespoon Worcestershire sauce
- 1 tablespoon Tabasco sauce
- ¼ teaspoon mustard powder
- ½ teaspoon ground black pepper
- 1 teaspoon xanthan gum
- 1 tablespoon cold water
- 1 pound cheddar cheese, shredded
- ¾ cup heavy whipping cream

How to Prepare

1. Heat a large-sized soup pan over medium-high heat and cook the bacon for about 8-10 minutes or until crisp.
2. With a slotted spoon, transfer the bacon onto a paper towel-lined plate to drain.
3. Crumble the bacon.
4. In the same pan with bacon grease, add the celery and onions over medium heat and sauté for about 6-7 minutes.
5. Add the broth and bring it to a boil.
6. Add the garlic, Worcestershire sauce, Tabasco sauce, mustard powder, and black pepper. Stir to combine.
7. Adjust the heat to low and simmer for about 4-5 minutes.
8. In a small-sized bowl, dissolve the glucomannan powder in cold water.
9. Add the water mixture into the broth mixture and stir to combine.
10. Add the cheddar cheese and heavy whipping cream and stir until smooth.
11. Serve hot with the garnishing of the reserved bacon.

Salmon & Vegetable Soup

Preparation time: 15 minutes
Cooking time: 30 minutes
Total time: 45 minutes
Servings: 4

Nutritional Values:

Calories 297, Total Fat 14.5 g, Saturated Fat 2.4 g,
Cholesterol 38 mg, Sodium 1011 mg, Total Carbs 18.5 g,
Fiber 5.7 g, Sugar 9.9 g, Protein 26.2 g

Ingredients

- 2 tablespoons olive oil
- 1 shallot, peeled and chopped
- 2 small garlic cloves, peeled and minced
- 1 jalapeño pepper, chopped
- 1 cabbage head, chopped
- 2 small bell peppers (red and yellow), seeded and chopped
- 5 cups vegetable broth
- 3 (4-ounce) boneless salmon fillets, cubed
- ¼ cup fresh cilantro, minced
- 2 tablespoons fresh lemon juice
- Salt and ground black pepper, as required
- 3 tablespoons fresh dill, chopped

How to Prepare

1. In a large-sized soup pan, heat oil over medium heat and sauté shallots and garlic for 2-3 minutes.
2. Add cabbage and bell peppers and sauté for about 3-4 minutes.
3. Add broth and bring it to a boil over high heat.
4. Adjust the heat to medium-low and simmer for about 10 minutes.
5. Add salmon and cook for about 5-6 minutes.
6. Stir in the cilantro, lemon juice, salt, and black pepper. Cook for about 1-2 minutes.
7. Serve hot with the topping of dill.

Shrimp Soup

Preparation time: 15 minutes
Cooking time: 30 minutes
Total time: 45 minutes
Servings: 6

Nutritional Values:

*Calories 404, Total Fat 29.7 g, Saturated Fat 23.6 g,
Cholesterol 159 mg, Sodium 990 mg, Total Carbs 9.8 g,
Fiber 0.8 g, Sugar 3.6 g, Protein 23.8 g*

Ingredients

- 1 tablespoon olive oil
- 1 small onion, peeled and chopped
- 1 tablespoon lemongrass, minced
- 1 tablespoon fresh ginger, peeled and minced
- 2 garlic cloves, peeled and minced
- 1 tablespoon red curry paste
- 3 cups chicken broth
- 1 tablespoon fish sauce
- 2 (14-ounce) cans full-fat coconut milk
- 8 ounces fresh shiitake mushrooms, cleaned and sliced
- 1-pound medium shrimp, peeled and deveined
- 1½ tablespoons fresh lime juice
- 2 teaspoons lime zest, grated
- Salt, as required

How to Prepare

1. In a large-sized soup pan, heat the oil over medium heat and sauté the onions for about 5-7 minutes.
2. Stir in the lemongrass, ginger, garlic, and curry paste. Sauté for about 1 minute.
3. Stir in the broth and fish sauce and simmer for about 10 minutes.
4. Add the coconut milk and stir to combine.
5. Add in the mushrooms and cook for about 5 minutes.
6. Add the shrimp and cook for about 5 minutes.
7. Stir in the lime juice, zest, and salt. Serve hot.

Beef Meatball Soup

Preparation time: 20 minutes
Cooking time: 25 minutes
Total time: 45 minutes
Servings: 6

Nutritional Values:

Calories 279, Total Fat 13.8 g, Saturated Fat 4.4 g,
Cholesterol 105 mg, Sodium 956 mg, Total Carbs 5 g,
Fiber 1.2 g, Sugar 2.2 g, Protein 33.4 g

Ingredients

Meatballs
- 1 pound ground beef
- ¼ cup Parmesan cheese, grated finely
- 1 large egg
- 2 teaspoons dried parsley
- 2 teaspoons dried basil
- 2 teaspoons dried oregano
- 2 teaspoons garlic powder
- 2 tablespoons olive oil

Soup
- 8 ounces fresh mushrooms, sliced
- 1 small onion, peeled and chopped finely
- 2 garlic cloves, peeled and crushed
- 6 cups chicken broth
- 2 cups fresh spinach, chopped
- Salt, as required
- ¼ cup Parmesan cheese, grated finely

How to Prepare

1. For the meatballs: in a bowl, add all ingredients except for oil. Mix until well combined.
2. Make small equal-sized balls from the mixture.
3. In a large-sized nonstick saucepan, heat the oil over medium-high heat and cook the meatballs for about 4-5 minutes or until browned.
4. With a slotted spoon, transfer the meatballs onto a plate and set aside.
5. In the same pan, add the mushrooms, onion, and garlic. Sauté for about 5-7 minutes.
6. Add the broth and cook for about 10 minutes.
7. Add in the meatballs cook for about 2-3 minutes.
8. Stir in the salt and remove from the heat.
9. Serve immediately with the garnishing of Parmesan cheese.

Ground Pork Soup

Preparation time: 15 minutes
Cooking time: 45 minutes
Total time: 1 hour
Servings: 8

Nutritional Values:

Calories 210, Total Fat 6.7 g, Saturated Fat 1.7 g,
Cholesterol 55 mg, Sodium 1211 mg, Total Carbs 10.8 g,
Fiber 3.4 g, Sugar 5.9 g, Protein 26.6 g

Ingredients

- 1 tablespoon olive oil
- 1 large onion, peeled and chopped
- 1 pound ground pork
- 2 garlic cloves, peeled and minced
- 1 teaspoon salt
- ½ teaspoon ground black pepper
- 6 cups cabbage, trimmed and shredded
- 1 (15-ounce) can diced tomatoes
- ½ teaspoon dried thyme
- ½ teaspoon dried oregano
- 1 bay leaf
- ½ teaspoon paprika
- 6 cups beef broth

How to Prepare

1. In a large-sized soup pan, heat the oil over medium-high heat and sauté the onions for about 3-5 minutes.
2. Add the ground pork, garlic, salt, and black pepper. Stir to combine.
3. Adjust the heat to medium-high and cook for about 7-8 minutes.
4. Add the cabbage, tomatoes, herbs, bay leaf, paprika, and broth. Bring it to a boil.
5. Adjust the heat to low and simmer for about 25 minutes.
6. Season with more salt and black pepper and serve hot.

Chicken & Tomato Soup

Preparation time: 15 minutes
Cooking time: 23 minutes
Total time: 38 minutes
Servings: 4

Nutritional Values:

Calories 218, Total Fat 12.5 g, Saturated Fat 2.8 g,
Cholesterol 27 mg, Sodium 834 mg, Total Carbs 10.3 g,
Fiber 4.9 g, Sugar 3.8 g, Protein 17.1 g

Ingredients

- 4 cups chicken broth
- 2 large tomatoes, peeled, seeded, and chopped
- 1 jalapeño pepper, seeded and minced
- 1 garlic clove, peeled and minced
- ½ teaspoon ground cumin
- 1 cup cooked chicken, shredded
- 3 scallions, trimmed and finely chopped
- Salt, as required
- ¼ cup fresh cilantro, chopped
- 2 tablespoons fresh lime juice
- 1 avocado, peeled, pitted, and chopped

How to Prepare

1. In a soup pan, add broth over medium heat and bring to a full rolling boil.
2. Add the tomatoes, jalapeño pepper, garlic, and cumin. Simmer for about 15 minutes.
3. Add the chicken, scallions, and salt. Stir to combine.
4. Adjust the heat to low and simmer for about 1-2 minutes.
5. Stir in the cilantro and lime juice. Remove the soup pan from heat.
6. Divide the avocado pieces into serving bowls and top with hot soup.
7. Serve immediately.

Mixed Spring Vegetable Soup

Preparation time: 15 minutes
Cooking time: 45 minutes
Total time: 1 hour
Servings: 8

Nutritional Values:

*Calories 154, Total Fat 4.5 g, Saturated Fat 0.9 g,
Cholesterol 0 mg, Sodium 836 mg, Total Carbs 19.3 g,
Fiber 6.3 g, Sugar 8.7 g, Protein 10.4 g*

Ingredients

- 1½ tablespoons olive oil
- 4 medium carrots, peeled and chopped
- 1 medium onion, peeled and chopped
- 2 celery stalks, trimmed and chopped
- 2 cups fresh tomatoes, chopped finely
- 3 cups small cauliflower florets
- 3 cups small broccoli florets
- 3 cups frozen green peas
- 8 cups vegetable broth
- 3 tablespoons fresh lemon juice
- Sea salt, as required

How to Prepare

1. In a large-sized soup pan, heat the oil over medium heat and sauté the carrots, celery, and onions for 6 minutes.
2. Stir in the garlic and sauté for about 1 minute.
3. Add the tomatoes and cook for about 2-3 minutes, crushing with the back of a spoon.
4. Add the vegetables and broth. Bring it to a boil over high heat.
5. Adjust the heat to low.
6. Cover the pan and simmer for about 30-35 minutes.
7. Mix in the lemon juice and salt. Remove from the heat.
8. Serve hot.

Asparagus Soup

Preparation time: 15 minutes
Cooking time: 40 minutes
Total time: 55 minutes
Servings: 4

Nutritional Values:

*Calories 108, Total Fat 5.2 g, Saturated Fat 1 g,
Cholesterol 0 mg, Sodium 809 mg, Total Carbs 8.5 g,
Fiber 3.9 g, Sugar 4.3 g, Protein 8.9 g*

Ingredients

- 1 tablespoon olive oil
- 3 scallions, trimmed and chopped
- 1½ pounds fresh asparagus, trimmed and chopped
- 4 cups vegetable broth
- 2 tablespoons fresh lemon juice
- Salt and ground black pepper, as required

How to Prepare

1. In a large-sized pan, heat the oil over medium heat and sauté the scallions for 4-5 minutes.
2. Stir in the asparagus and broth. Bring it to a boil.
3. Adjust the heat to low and simmer, covered, for 25-30 minutes.
4. Remove from the heat and set aside to cool slightly.
5. Transfer the soup into a high-powered blender in 2 batches and pulse until smooth.
6. Return the soup into the same pan over medium heat and simmer for 4-5 minutes.
7. Stir in the lemon juice, salt, and black pepper. Remove from the heat.
8. Serve hot.

30-Minute Spinach Soup

Preparation time: 15 minutes
Cooking time: 5 minutes
Total time: 20 minutes
Servings: 3

Nutritional Values:

*Calories 154, Total Fat 4.5 g, Saturated Fat 0.9 g,
Cholesterol 0 mg, Sodium 836 mg, Total Carbs 19.3 g,
Fiber 6.3 g, Sugar 8.7 g, Protein 10.4 g*

Ingredients

- 6 cups fresh spinach, chopped
- 2 garlic cloves, peeled
- 2 cups water
- 1 cup unsweetened coconut milk
- 1 tablespoon fresh lime juice
- ½ teaspoon cayenne powder
- Salt and ground black pepper, as required

How to Prepare

1. Place all soup ingredients in a high-powered blender and pulse on high speed until smooth.
2. Transfer the soup into a pan over medium heat and cook for about 3-5 minutes or until heated through.
3. Serve hot.

30-Minute Tomato Soup

Preparation time: 10 minutes
Cooking time: 15 minutes
Total time: 25 minutes
Servings: 4

Nutritional Values:

*Calories 108, Total Fat 3 g, Saturated Fat 0.4 g,
Cholesterol 0 mg, Sodium 81 mg, Total Carbs 19.5 g,
Fiber 4.2 g, Sugar 13.8 g, Protein 4.3 g*

Ingredients

- 2 teaspoons olive oil
- 1 medium white onion, peeled and chopped
- 3 garlic cloves, peeled and minced
- 7 cups fresh plum tomatoes, chopped
- ½ cup fresh basil, chopped
- Salt and ground black pepper, as required
- ¼ teaspoon cayenne powder

How to Prepare

1. In a pan, heat the oil over medium heat and sauté the onions and garlic for about 5-6 minutes.
2. Add the tomatoes and cook for about 6-8 minutes, crushing with the back of spoon occasionally.
3. Stir in the basil, salt, and cayenne powder. Remove from the heat.
4. With a hand blender, puree the soup mixture until smooth.
5. Serve immediately.

Noodles & Chicken Soup

Preparation time: 20 minutes
Cooking time: 35 minutes
Total time: 55 minutes
Servings: 8

Nutritional Values:

Calories 329, Total Fat 15 g, Saturated Fat 4.4 g,
Cholesterol 96 mg, Sodium 811 mg, Total Carbs 14.8 g,
Fiber 1.2 g, Sugar 2 g, Protein 31.8 g

Ingredients

- 6 (4-ounce) bone-in, skinless chicken breasts
- Salt and ground black pepper, as required
- 2 tablespoons canola oil
- 2 tablespoons unsalted butter
- 1 medium onion, peeled and chopped
- 6 garlic cloves, peeled and minced
- 2 celery stalks, trimmed and sliced
- 1 large carrot, trimmed, peeled, and sliced thinly
- 8 cups chicken broth
- ¾ teaspoon dried parsley
- ¾ teaspoon dried thyme
- ¾ teaspoon dried basil
- ¼ teaspoon red pepper flakes, crushed
- 12 ounces wide egg noodles
- ¼ cup fresh parsley, chopped

How to Prepare

1. Season the chicken breasts with salt and black pepper.
2. In a large-sized-sized Dutch oven, heat the oil over medium heat and cook the chicken breasts for about 2 minutes per side.
3. With a slotted spoon, transfer the chicken breasts onto a plate.
4. In the same pan, melt the butter over medium heat and sauté the onions for about 2 minutes.
5. Add the garlic and sauté for about 1 minute.
6. Add the celery and carrots. Cook for about 5-7 minutes, stirring occasionally.
7. Add the dried herbs and red pepper flakes. Cook for about 1 minute.
8. Stir in the cooked chicken and broth. Bring it to a boil.
9. Cover the pan and cook for about 5 minutes.
10. With tongs, transfer the chicken breasts onto a plate.
11. Into the pan, stir in the noodles and bring it to a boil
12. Cook for about 10 minutes.
13. Meanwhile, remove the bones from the chicken breasts and, with a fork, shred the meat.
14. Add the shredded meat back into the Dutch oven and stir to combine.
15. Cook for about 1-2 minutes.
16. Stir in the salt and black pepper and remove from the heat.
17. Serve hot with the garnishing of fresh parsley.

Pasta & Vegetable Soup

Preparation time: 15 minutes
Cooking time: 20 minutes
Total time: 35 minutes
Servings: 4

Nutritional Values:

Calories 167, Total Fat 8.8 g, Saturated Fat 1 g,
Cholesterol 10 mg, Sodium 843 mg, Total Carbs 14.5 g,
Fiber 1.6 g, Sugar 3.3 g, Protein 7.2 g

Ingredients

- 2 tablespoons canola oil
- 1 cup celery, trimmed and sliced
- ¾ cup carrot, peeled and sliced
- 1 medium onion, peeled and chopped
- 1 garlic clove, peeled and smashed
- Salt, as required
- ½ cup pasta
- 4 cups vegetable broth
- 2 tablespoons fresh parsley, chopped
- 1 tablespoon fresh lemon juice
- Ground black pepper, as required

How to Prepare

1. In a large-sized-sized soup pan, heat oil over medium heat and cook the celery, carrots, onions, garlic, and salt for about 4-5 minutes, stirring frequently.
2. Add the pasta and cook for about 2 minutes, stirring continuously.
3. Add in broth and stir to combine.
4. Adjust the heat to high and bring to a full rolling boil.
5. Immediately cover the soup pan and cook for about 8 minutes.
6. Stir in parsley, lemon juice, salt, and black pepper. Serve.

This page is for your notes

This page is for your notes

This page is for your notes

This page is for your notes

This page is for your notes

Summer Soups

Classic Chilled Yogurt Soup

Preparation time: 15 minutes
Total time: 15 minutes
Servings: 6

Nutritional Values:

*Calories 166, Total Fat 7.2 g, Saturated Fat 2.4 g,
Cholesterol 11 mg, Sodium 139 mg, Total Carbs 15 g,
Fiber 0.8 g, Sugar 11.7 g, Protein 9.4 g*

Ingredients

- 3 cups plain Greek yogurt
- 1-2 cups milk
- 2 tablespoons extra-virgin olive oil
- 1-pound Persian cucumbers, grated
- 1/3 cup fresh dill, chopped
- 1 teaspoon garlic, crushed
- Salt and ground white pepper, as required

How to Prepare

1. In a large-sized bowl, add the yogurt, milk, and oil. Whisk until well combined.
2. Grate the Persian cucumbers into a separate bowl.
3. Wrap the grated cucumbers in a cheesecloth and squeeze to remove excess liquid.
4. Into the bowl of yogurt mixture, add the cucumbers, dill, garlic, salt, and white pepper. Stir to blend.
5. Place the bowl in refrigerator to chill for 3-4 hours.
6. Just before serving, stir the mixture well.

Classic Strawberry Gazpacho

Preparation time: 15 minutes
Total time: 15 minutes
Servings: 6

Nutritional Values:

*Calories 178, Total Fat 1.5 g, Saturated Fat 0.8 g,
Cholesterol 5 mg, Sodium 59 mg, Total Carbs 36.2 g,
Fiber 3.1 g, Sugar 31.6 g, Protein 5.8 g*

Ingredients

- 2 cups vanilla yogurt
- ½ cup fresh orange juice
- 2 pounds fresh strawberries, hull and halved
- ½ cup sugar

How to Prepare

1. Add all the ingredients into a high-powered blender and pulse until smooth.
2. Transfer the soup into a large-sized bowl.
3. Cover the bowl and refrigerate to chill for at least 2-3 hours before serving. Garnish with slices of fresh strawberries.

Classic Chicken & Mushroom Soup

Preparation time: 15 minutes
Cooking time: 30 minutes
Total time: 45 minutes
Servings: 6

Nutritional Values:

Calories 369, Total Fat 26.4 g, Saturated Fat 19.6 g,
Cholesterol 59 mg, Sodium 611 mg, Total Carbs 9.4 g,
Fiber 3.1 g, Sugar 4.9 g, Protein 26 g

Ingredients

- 1 tablespoon coconut oil
- 1 large onion, peeled and chopped
- 4 cups fresh mushrooms, cleaned, trimmed, and sliced thinly
- 1 celery stalk, trimmed and chopped
- 14 ounces boneless, skinless chicken breasts, cubed
- 4 cups chicken broth
- 1 tablespoon curry powder
- 16 ounces coconut milk
- Salt and ground black pepper, as required

How to Prepare

1. In a large-sized soup pan, heat oil over medium heat and sauté onions, mushrooms, and celery for about 5 minutes.
2. Add chicken, broth, and curry powder. Bring to a full rolling boil.
3. Adjust the heat to low and simmer for about 10 minutes.
4. Add in coconut milk and stir to combine.
5. Adjust the heat to high and bring to a full rolling boil.
6. Adjust the heat to low and simmer for about 3-4 minutes.
7. Add in salt and black pepper and serve hot.

Classic Cauliflower Soup

Preparation time: 10 minutes
Cooking time: 25 minutes
Total time: 35 minutes
Servings: 4

Nutritional Values:

Calories 285, Total Fat 23 g, Saturated Fat 14.1 g,
Cholesterol 0 mg, Sodium 861 mg, Total Carbs 14.9 g,
Fiber 4.8 g, Sugar 7.2 g, Protein 8.5 g

Ingredients

- 2 tablespoons olive oil
- 1 yellow onion, peeled and chopped
- 2 carrots, peeled and chopped
- 2 celery stalks, trimmed and chopped
- 2 garlic cloves, peeled and minced
- 1 Serrano pepper, chopped finely
- 1 teaspoon ground turmeric
- 1 teaspoon ground coriander
- 1 teaspoon ground cumin
- ¼ teaspoon red pepper flakes, crushed
- 1 head cauliflower, chopped
- 4 cups vegetable broth
- 1 cup coconut milk
- Salt and ground black pepper, as required
- 2 tablespoons fresh chives, chopped

How to Prepare

1. In a large-sized saucepan, heat the oil over medium heat and sauté the onions, carrots, and celery for 5-6 minutes.
2. Add the garlic, Serrano pepper, and spices. Sauté for about 1 minute.
3. Add the cauliflower and cook for 5 minutes, stirring occasionally.
4. Add the broth and coconut milk. Bring it to a boil over medium-high heat.
5. Adjust the heat to low and simmer for about 15 minutes.
6. Season the soup with salt and black pepper. Remove from the heat.
7. Serve hot with a topping of chives.

Creamy Tomato Soup

Preparation time: 15 minutes
Cooking time: 20 minutes
Total time: 35 minutes
Servings: 5

Nutritional Values:

*Calories 123, Total Fat 5.9 g, Saturated Fat 2 g, Cholestero
18 mg, Sodium 679 mg, Total Carbs 12.3 g, Fiber 3.8 g,
Sugar 7.7 g, Protein 6.1 g*

Ingredients

- 1 tablespoon olive oil
- 1 small yellow onion, peeled and sliced thinly
- 3 garlic cloves, peeled and chopped
- 4 tablespoons sugar-free tomato paste
- 1 (16-ounce) can crushed tomatoes
- 3 cups chicken broth
- ¼ cup heavy cream
- Salt and ground black pepper, as required
- 2-3 tablespoons fresh basil leaves

How to Prepare

1. In a large-sized soup pan, heat olive oil over medium-high heat and sauté the onions for about 2-3 minutes.
2. Add the garlic and sauté for about 1 minute.
3. Add the tomato paste and stir to combine.
4. Stir in the broth, tomatoes, heavy cream, salt, and black pepper. Simmer for about 15 minutes.
5. Remove from the heat and, with an immersion blender, blend the soup until smooth.
6. Garnish with basil and serve immediately.

Cheesy & Creamy Broccoli Soup

Preparation time: 15 minutes
Cooking time: 35 minutes
Total time: 50 minutes
Servings: 6

Nutritional Values:

*Calories 443, Total Fat 38.4 g, Saturated Fat 23.7 g,
Cholesterol 119 mg, Sodium 1011 mg, Total Carbs 10.3 g,
Fiber 3.2 g, Sugar 2.4 g, Protein 16.3 g*

Ingredients

- 8 ounces cream cheese
- 2 tablespoons butter
- 1 teaspoon paprika
- 1 teaspoon onion powder
- ½ teaspoon garlic powder
- 4½ cups chicken broth
- 1 cup heavy whipping cream
- 16 ounces frozen chopped broccoli
- 1 cup sharp cheddar cheese, shredded

How to Prepare

1. In a heavy-bottomed soup pan, add the cream cheese, butter, paprika, onion powder, and garlic powder over medium heat and cook for about 2-3 minutes, stirring frequently.
2. Add the broth and heavy cream. Stir to combine.
3. Adjust the heat to medium-high and bring it to a boil, stirring occasionally.
4. Cook for about 5-8 minutes, stirring occasionally.
5. Stir in the broccoli and again bring to a boil.
6. Adjust the heat to low and simmer, covered, for about 20 minutes.
7. Remove from the heat and stir in the cheddar cheese, salt, and black pepper.
8. With an immersion blender, blend the soup until smooth.
9. Serve immediately.

Creamy Lobster Soup

Preparation time: 15 minutes
Cooking time: 25 minutes
Total time: 40 minutes
Servings: 6

Nutritional Values:

*Calories 255, Total Fat 13.3 g, Saturated Fat 6.6 g,
Cholesterol 141 mg, Sodium 1122 mg, Total Carbs 7.7 g,
Fiber 1.2 g, Sugar 3.1 g, Protein 18.6 g*

Ingredients

Soup
- 1 tablespoon olive oil
- 2 carrots, peeled and chopped
- 2 celery stalks, trimmed and chopped
- 1 small onion, peeled and chopped
- 4 garlic cloves, minced
- 32 ounces seafood broth
- 1 cup dry white wine
- 2 tablespoons tomato paste
- 2 teaspoons Old Bay seasoning
- ¾ cup heavy cream

Lobster
- 2 tablespoons butter
- 16 ounces uncooked lobster claw meat
- 3-4 garlic cloves
- 1 tablespoon fresh lemon juice

How to Prepare

1. For the soup: in a large-sized soup pan, heat the olive oil over medium heat and sauté the carrots, celery, onions, and garlic for about 4-5 minutes.
2. Add the broth, wine, tomato paste, and Old Bay seasoning. Bring it to a boil.
3. Simmer for about 15 minutes.
4. Remove from the heat and, with an immersion blender, blend the soup until smooth.
5. Stir in the heavy cream and return the pan over low heat.
6. Cover the pan to keep the soup hot.
7. In a skillet, melt the butter over medium heat and sauté the lobster meat with garlic and lemon juice for about 3-4 minutes.
8. Transfer the lobster mixture into the pan of soup and stir to combine.
9. Serve hot.

Salmon & Potato Soup

Preparation time: 15 minutes
Cooking time: 35 minutes
Total time: 50 minutes
Servings: 8

Nutritional Values:

Calories 446, Total Fat 24.6 g, Saturated Fat 11.8 g,
Cholesterol 104 mg, Sodium 682 mg, Total Carbs 23.3 g,
Fiber 2.3 g, Sugar 8.1 g, Protein 35.1 g

Ingredients

- 3 tablespoons unsalted butter
- ¾ cup onion, peeled and chopped
- ½ cup celery, trimmed and chopped
- 1 teaspoon garlic powder
- 2 cups potatoes, cleaned and chopped
- 2 carrots, peeled and chopped
- 1 teaspoon dried dill weed
- 2 cups chicken broth
- Salt and ground black pepper, as required
- 2 (16-ounce) cans salmon
- 1 (15-ounce) can creamed corn
- ½ pound cheddar cheese, shredded
- 1 (12-ounce) can evaporated milk

How to Prepare

1. In a large-sized-sized soup pan, melt butter over medium heat and sauté onions, celery, and garlic powder for about 4-5 minutes.
2. Add the potatoes, carrots, broth, dill, salt, and black pepper. Stir to combine.
3. Adjust the heat to high and bring to a full rolling boil.
4. Adjust the heat to low and simmer, covered, for about 20 minutes.
5. Stir in salmon, corn, cheese, and evaporated milk. Cook for about 4-5 minutes, stirring frequently.
6. Serve hot.

Halibut & Scallion Soup

Preparation time: 15 minutes
Cooking time: 37 minutes
Total time: 53 minutes
Servings: 4

Nutritional Values:

Calories 324, Total Fat 11.1 g, Saturated Fat 2.2 g,
Cholesterol 79 mg, Sodium 1790 mg, Total Carbs 56.8 g,
Fiber 1.7 g, Sugar 3.8 g, Protein 46.9 g

Ingredients

- 1 teaspoon olive oil
- ¼ cup fresh parsley, chopped
- 2 garlic cloves, peeled and minced
- 3 tomatoes, chopped
- 10 canned oil-packed anchovies, minced
- 1 teaspoon red pepper flakes, crushed
- Salt and ground black pepper, as required
- 6 cups vegetable broth
- 1 pound halibut fillets, chopped
- 3-4 scallions, trimmed and chopped

How to Prepare

1. In a large-sized soup pan, heat olive oil over medium heat and sauté the parsley and garlic for about 1 minute.
2. Add the tomatoes, anchovies, red pepper flakes, salt, black pepper, and broth. Stir to combine.
3. Adjust the heat to high and bring it to a boil.
4. Adjust the heat to medium-low and simmer, covered, for about 20 minutes.
5. Add in the halibut and scallions and cook, covered, for about 8-10 minutes.
6. Serve hot.

Beef & Vegetable Soup

Preparation time: 15 minutes
Cooking time: 30 minutes
Total time: 45 minutes
Servings: 3

Nutritional Values:

Calories 306, Total Fat 17.3 g, Saturated Fat 4.4 g,
Cholesterol 42 mg, Sodium 9171 mg, Total Carbs 10.3 g,
Fiber 1.8 g, Sugar 3.1 g, Protein 27.9 g

Ingredients

- 2 tablespoons olive oil, divided
- 1 garlic clove, peeled and minced
- 8-ounce flank steak, trimmed and cubed
- Salt and ground black pepper, as required
- 1 teaspoon fresh rosemary, stemmed and chopped
- ¼ teaspoon red pepper flakes, crushed
- ¾ cup fresh shiitake mushrooms, cleaned and sliced
- 1 small yellow squash, trimmed and chopped
- ¾ cup fresh kale leaves, tough ribs removed and torn into pieces
- 3 cups beef broth
- 1 tablespoon low-sodium soy sauce
- 2 tablespoons scallion, trimmed and chopped
- ½ tablespoon fresh lime juice

How to Prepare

1. In a Dutch oven, heat 1 tablespoon of the oil over medium heat and sauté the garlic for about 1 minute.
2. Add the beef with salt and black pepper. Cook for about 4-5 minutes or until browned.
3. Transfer the beef into a bowl.
4. In the same pan, heat the remaining oil over medium heat and sauté the rosemary and red pepper flakes for about 1 minute.
5. Add the mushrooms, yellow squash, and kale. Cook for about 2-3 minutes.
6. Add the cooked beef and broth. Bring it to a boil.
7. Adjust the heat to low and simmer for about 10-15 minutes
8. Add the soy sauce and simmer for about 5 minutes more.
9. Stir in scallions, lemon juice, salt, and black pepper. Remove from heat.
10. Serve hot.

43

Ham & Split Peas Soup

Preparation time: 15 minutes
Cooking time: 1½ hours
Total time: 1¾ hours
Servings: 8

Nutritional Values:

Calories 336, Total Fat 9.1 g, Saturated Fat 3.8 g,
Cholesterol 40 mg, Sodium 1171 mg, Total Carbs 38 g,
Fiber 15.4 g, Sugar 5.3 g, Protein 26 g

Ingredients

- 2 tablespoons unsalted butter
- 2 celery stalks, trimmed and chopped
- ½ onion, peeled and chopped
- 3 garlic cloves, peeled and sliced
- 1 pound ham, chopped
- 1-pound dried split peas, rinsed
- 1 bay leaf
- 4 cups chicken broth
- 2½ cup water
- Salt and ground black pepper, as required

How to Prepare

1. In a large-sized-sized soup pan, melt butter over medium-low heat and cook the celery, onions, and garlic for about 9-10 minutes, stirring frequently.
2. Add ham, split peas, bay leaf, broth, and water. Stir to combine.
3. Adjust the heat to high and bring it to a boil.
4. Adjust the heat to low and simmer, covered, for about 1½ hours, stirring occasionally.
5. Stir in salt and black pepper. Serve hot.

Chicken & Potato Soup

Preparation time: 15 minutes
Cooking time: 50 minutes
Total time: 1 hour 5 minutes
Servings: 10

Nutritional Values:

Calories 301, Total Fat 10.3 g, Saturated Fat 2.2 g,
Cholesterol 61 mg, Sodium 385 mg, Total Carbs 27.3 g,
Fiber 6 g, Sugar 6.1 g, Protein 25.2 g

Ingredients

- 3 tablespoons olive oil
- 4 (6-ounce) boneless, skinless chicken breasts
- 2 large onions, peeled and chopped
- 4 garlic cloves, peeled and minced
- 1 tablespoon fresh ginger, peeled and grated
- 2 large potatoes, peeled and chopped
- 4 parsnips, peeled and chopped
- 2 zucchinis, chopped
- 2 teaspoons ground cumin
- 1 teaspoon ground turmeric
- 4 cups chicken broth
- 6 cups water
- 1 cup fresh green peas, shelled
- 1 cup fresh cilantro, chopped

How to Prepare

1. In a large-sized-sized soup pan, heat oil over medium heat and cook the chicken breasts for about 4-5 minutes.
2. With a slotted spoon, transfer the chicken breasts onto a plate.
3. Into the same soup pan, add the onions and sauté for about 3-4 minutes.
4. Add the garlic and ginger. Sauté for about 1 minute.
5. Stir in potatoes, parsnips, and zucchini. Cook for about 5 minutes, stirring occasionally.
6. Stir in cooked chicken, spices, salt, black pepper, broth, and water. Bring to a full rolling boil.
7. Adjust the heat to medium-low and simmer for about 10-15 minutes.
8. With a slotted spoon, transfer the chicken breasts into a bowl.
9. With 2 forks, shred the meat.
10. Return the shredded meat and peas into the soup pan. Simmer for about 10-15 minutes.
11. Serve hot with the garnishing of cilantro.

Potato & Asparagus Soup

Preparation time: 15 minutes
Cooking time: 30 minutes
Total time: 45 minutes
Servings: 6

Nutritional Values:

*Calories 186, Total Fat 4 g, Saturated Fat 0.8 g,
Cholesterol 0 mg, Sodium 811 mg, Total Carbs 30.1 g,
Fiber 3.7 g, Sugar 5.4 g, Protein 8.6 g*

Ingredients

- 1 tablespoon olive oil
- 1 large carrot, peeled and chopped
- 1 small bell pepper, chopped
- 1 leek (white portion), cut into ¼-inch slices
- 2 garlic cloves, peeled and minced
- 10 baby red potatoes, cubed
- 6 cups chicken broth
- 8-10 fresh asparagus spears, cut into 1-inch pieces
- 1 teaspoon sugar
- Salt and ground black pepper, as required

How to Prepare

1. In a large-sized saucepan, heat the oil over medium heat and sauté the carrot, bell pepper, and leek for about 3-4 minutes.
2. Add garlic and cook for about 1 minute.
3. Stir in the potatoes and broth. Bring it to a boil.
4. Reduce heat to low and cook, covered, for about 8-10 minutes.
5. Stir in the asparagus, sugar, salt, and black pepper. Cook, covered, for about 8-10 minutes.
6. Serve hot.

White Beans & Spinach Soup

Preparation time: 5 minutes
Cooking time: 55 minutes
Total time: 1 hour 5 minutes
Servings: 4

Nutritional Values:

Calories 270, Total Fat 3.3 g, Saturated Fat 0.5 g,
Cholesterol 0 mg, Sodium 324 mg, Total Carbs 50.3 g,
Fiber 15.3 g, Sugar 3 g, Protein 11.8 g

Ingredients

- 2 teaspoons olive oil
- 1 medium onion, peeled and chopped
- 4 garlic cloves, peeled and minced
- 2 teaspoons fresh rosemary leaves, minced
- 1-pound white potatoes, peeled and cut into small cubes
- 4 cups water
- Salt and ground black pepper, as required
- 1 (15-ounce) can white beans, rinsed and drained
- 3 cups fresh spinach, chopped roughly

How to Prepare

1. In a large-sized pan, heat the oil over medium heat and cook the onions for about 5-7 minutes, stirring frequently.
2. Add the garlic and rosemary and sauté for about 1 minute.
3. Add the potatoes, water, salt, and black pepper. Bring it to a boil.
4. Adjust the heat to low and simmer, uncovered, for about 30-35 minutes.
5. With the back of a spoon, mash some of the potatoes roughly.
6. Stir in the beans and spinach. Simmer for about 5-7 minutes.
7. Serve hot.

30-Minute Zucchini Soup

Preparation time: 15 minutes
Cooking time: 4 minutes
Total time: 19 minutes
Servings: 2

Nutritional Values:

*Calories 200, Total Fat 15.8g, Saturated Fat 6 g,
Cholesterol 30 mg, Sodium 732 mg, Total Carbs 6.2 g,
Fiber 1.5 g, Sugar 3 g, Protein 8 g*

Ingredients

- In a microwave-safe bowl, add the zucchini and dried onions. Microwave on high for about 4 minutes.
- Meanwhile, in a bowl, dissolve the Better than Bouillon in boiling water
- Transfer the zucchini into a high-powered blender and pulse until chopped finely.
- In the blender, add the water mixture, cheese, oil, thyme, salt, and black pepper. Pulse until smooth and creamy.
- Serve immediately.

How to Prepare

1. In a microwave-safe bowl, add the zucchini and dried onions. Microwave on high for about 4 minutes.
2. Meanwhile, in a bowl, dissolve the Better than Bouillon in boiling water
3. Transfer the zucchini into a high-powered blender and pulse until chopped finely.
4. In the blender, add the water mixture, cheese, oil, thyme, salt, and black pepper. Pulse until smooth and creamy.
5. Serve immediately.

30-Minute Beet Soup

Preparation time: 15 minutes
Cooking time: 5 minutes
Total time: 20 minutes
Servings: 2

Nutritional Values:

Calories 317, Total Fat 8.7 g, Saturated Fat 4.6 g,
Cholesterol 20 mg, Sodium 396 mg, Total Carbs 37.4 g,
Fiber 4.1 g, Sugar 31 g, Protein 19.3 g

Ingredients

- 2 cups plain yogurt
- 4 teaspoons fresh lemon juice
- 2 cups beets, trimmed, peeled, and chopped
- 2 tablespoons fresh dill
- Salt, as required
- 1 tablespoon pumpkin seeds
- 2 tablespoons sour cream
- 1 tablespoon fresh chives, minced

How to Prepare

1. In a high-powered blender, add all ingredients and pulse until smooth.
2. Transfer the soup into a pan over medium heat and cook for about 3-5 minutes or until heated through.
3. Serve immediately with the garnishing of chives and cream.

Pasta & Zucchini Soup

Preparation time: 15 minutes
Cooking time: 25 minutes
Total time: 40 minutes
Servings: 4

Nutritional Values:

*Calories 144, Total Fat 8.7 g, Saturated Fat 1 g,
Cholesterol 7 mg, Sodium 819 mg, Total Carbs 9.6 g,
Fiber 1.2 g, Sugar 2 g, Protein 6.7 g*

Ingredients

- 2 tablespoons canola oil
- ¼ cup celery, trimmed and sliced
- ¼ cup carrot, peeled and sliced
- ¼ cup onion, peeled and chopped
- 1 garlic clove, peeled and smashed
- Salt, as required
- 1/3 cup shell pasta
- ½ cup zucchini, chopped
- ½ cup green beans, trimmed and chopped
- 4 cups vegetable broth
- 2 tablespoons fresh parsley, chopped
- 1 tablespoon fresh lemon juice
- Ground black pepper, as required

How to Prepare

1. In a large-sized-sized soup pan, heat oil over medium heat and cook the celery, carrots, onions, garlic, and salt for about 6 minutes, stirring frequently.
2. Add the pasta and cook for about 2 minutes, stirring continuously.
3. Add in zucchini, green beans, and broth. Stir to combine.
4. Adjust the heat to high and bring to a full rolling boil.
5. Immediately cover the soup pan and cook for about 8-10 minutes.
6. Stir in parsley, lemon juice, salt, and black pepper. Serve.

Tortellini & Spinach Soup

Preparation time: 15 minutes
Cooking time: 25 minutes
Total time: 40 minutes
Servings: 8

Nutritional Values:

*Calories 192, Total Fat 7.1 g, Saturated Fat 0.9 g,
Cholesterol 7 mg, Sodium 704 mg, Total Carbs 23.9 g,
Fiber 2.1 g, Sugar 3.9 g, Protein 9.3 g*

Ingredients

- 2 tablespoons olive oil
- 1 medium onion, peeled and chopped finely
- 3 garlic cloves, peeled and minced
- 1 (49½-ounce) can chicken broth
- 2 teaspoons Italian seasoning
- 1 (9-ounce) package refrigerated cheese tortellini
- 1 (28-ounce) can crushed tomatoes with juices
- 8 ounces fresh spinach, chopped
- Salt and ground black pepper, as required

How to Prepare

1. Heat the oil in a large-sized-sized Dutch oven over medium heat, add the onions and cook for about 3-4 minutes, stirring continuously.
2. Add garlic and cook for about 1 minute, stirring continuously.
3. Add broth and Italian seasoning. Bring it to a boil.
4. Cook for about 5 minutes.
5. Meanwhile, cook tortellini according to package's directions
6. Drain the tortellini.
7. Add the cooked tortellini and tomatoes into soup mixture and cook for about 5 minutes.
8. Add spinach and cook for about 3-5 minutes.
9. Season with salt and black pepper. Serve hot.

This page is for your notes

This page is for your notes

This page is for your notes

This page is for your notes

This page is for your notes

Fall Soups

Classic Pumpkin Soup

Preparation time: 15 minutes
Cooking time: 25 minutes
Total time: 40 minutes
Servings: 4

Nutritional Values:

Calories 139, Total Fat 4.4 g, Saturated Fat 1 g,
Cholesterol 0 mg, Sodium 861 mg, Total Carbs 19.3 g,
Fiber 6 g, Sugar 8 g, Protein 7.6 g

Ingredients

- 2 teaspoons olive oil
- 1 onion, peeled and chopped
- 1 teaspoon fresh ginger, peeled and chopped
- 2 garlic cloves, peeled and chopped
- 2 tablespoons fresh cilantro, chopped
- 3 cups pumpkin, peeled and chopped finely
- 4¼ cups vegetable broth
- Salt and ground black pepper, as required
- 2 tablespoons fresh lime juice

How to Prepare

1. In a large-sized soup pan, heat oil over medium heat and sauté the onions, turmeric, ginger, garlic, and cilantro for about 3-5 minutes.
2. Add the pumpkin and broth. Bring to a boil
3. Turn the heat to low and simmer, covered, for about 15 minutes.
4. Remove from heat and, with an immersion blender, puree the soup until smooth.
5. Drizzle with lime juice and serve hot.

Classic Squash & Apple Soup

Preparation time: 15 minutes
Cooking time: 45 minutes
Total time: 1 hour
Servings: 4

Nutritional Values:

Calories 129, Total Fat 1.3 g, Saturated Fat 0.2 g,
Cholesterol 0mg, Sodium 46 mg, Total Carbs 31.4 g,
Fiber 5.9 g, Sugar 15.2 g, Protein 1.9 g

Ingredients

- 2 tablespoon avocado oil
- 1 cup white onion, peeled and chopped
- 2 garlic cloves, peeled and minced
- 1 teaspoon dried thyme
- 3 cups butternut squash, peeled and cubed
- 2 apples, cored and chopped
- 4 cups water
- Sea salt, as required

How to Prepare

1. In a soup pan, heat avocado oil over medium heat and sauté the onions for about 5 minutes.
2. Add the garlic and thyme. Sauté for about 1 minute.
3. Add the squash, apple, and ginger. Cook for about 1-2 minutes.
4. Stir in the water and bring it to a boil.
5. Adjust the heat to low and simmer, covered, for about 30 minutes.
6. Stir in the salt and remove from the heat.
7. With a hand blender, puree the soup mixture until smooth.
8. Serve immediately.

Classic Bean & Pumpkin Soup

Preparation time: 15 minutes
Cooking time: 40 minutes
Total time: 55 minutes
Servings: 6

Nutritional Values:

Calories 294, Total Fat 6.6 g, Saturated Fat 1.3 g,
Cholesterol 1 mg, Sodium 302 mg, Total Carbs 45 g,
Fiber1 5.6 g, Sugar 5.1 g, Protein 16.4 g

Ingredients

- 2 tablespoons olive oil
- 1 medium onion, peeled and chopped
- 4 garlic cloves, peeled and minced
- 1 tablespoon ground cumin
- 1 teaspoon red chili powder
- Salt and ground black pepper, as required
- 2 (15-ounce) cans black beans, drained
- 1 (16-ounce) can pumpkin puree
- 1 cup tomatoes, finely chopped
- 2 cups chicken broth
- ¼ cup plain Greek yogurt

How to Prepare

1. In a large-sized soup pan, heat oil over medium heat and sauté the onions for about 6-8 minutes.
2. Add in garlic, cumin, chili powder, and black pepper. Sauté for about 1 minute.
3. Add the black beans, pumpkin, tomatoes, and broth. Stir to combine.
4. Adjust the heat to medium-high and bring to a full rolling boil.
5. Adjust the heat and simmer, uncovered, for about 25 minutes, stirring occasionally.
6. Remove the soup pan from heat and stir in yogurt.
7. With an immersion blender, blend the soup slightly.
8. Serve hot with the garnishing of cilantro.

Classic Turkey & Rice Soup

Preparation time: 20 minutes
Cooking time: 2 hours 5 minutes
Total time: 2 hours 25 minutes
Servings: 6

Nutritional Values:

Calories 498, Total Fat 24.3 g, Saturated Fat 13.3 g,
Cholesterol 126 mg, Sodium 602 mg, Total Carbs 33.4 g,
Fiber 3.3 g, Sugar 3.5 g, Protein 37 g

Ingredients

- 2 smoked turkey legs
- 1 cup baby carrots, peeled and sliced
- 1 onion, peeled and chopped
- 2 cups celery stalks, trimmed and chopped
- 2 garlic cloves, peeled and minced
- 2 bay leaves
- 1 teaspoon dried marjoram, crushed
- 1 teaspoon dried thyme, crushed
- 1 tablespoon onion powder
- 1 tablespoon garlic powder
- 2 teaspoons ground black pepper
- 1 teaspoon curry powder
- 4 chicken bouillon cubes
- 8 cups water
- 1 cup uncooked wild rice
- 4 cups half-and-half

How to Prepare

1. In a large-sized soup pan, add all ingredients, except rice and half-and-half, over high heat and bring it to a boil. Adjust the heat to low and simmer for about 30 minutes.
2. Stir in rice and simmer for about 1 hour.
3. Transfer the turkey legs into a large-sized bowl and let them cool.
4. Pull the meat from bones and then chop it.
5. Stir in half-and-half and turkey meat. Simmer for about 30 minutes.
6. Serve hot.

Creamy Butternut Squash Soup

Preparation time: 15 minutes
Cooking time: 40 minutes
Total time: 55 minutes
Servings: 6

Nutritional Values:

*Calories 382, Total Fat 26.7 g, Saturated Fat 8.1 g,
Cholesterol 27 mg, Sodium 684mg, Total Carbs 31 g,
Fiber 4.7 g, Sugar 6.2 g, Protein 10.1 g*

Ingredients

- 3 tablespoons olive oil
- 1 large onion, peeled and chopped finely
- 1 cup raw cashews
- 1 garlic clove, peeled and minced
- 2 tablespoons fresh ginger, peeled and minced
- 1 (2-pound) butternut squash, peeled and cubed into ½-inch size
- 2 teaspoons ground coriander
- 2 teaspoons ground cumin
- 1 teaspoon ground turmeric
- 1 teaspoon curry powder
- Salt and ground black pepper, as required
- 5 cups vegetable broth
- 1 cup heavy cream

How to Prepare

1. In a large-sized soup pan, heat oil over medium heat and sauté the onions for about 5 minutes.
2. Add cashews and sauté for about 3 minutes.
3. Add garlic and ginger. Sauté for about 30-60 seconds.
4. Add remaining ingredients, except for cream, and bring it to a boil
5. Adjust the heat to low and cook, covered, for about 20-25 minutes.
6. Remove from heat and stir in cream.
7. With a hand blender, puree the soup mixture until smooth.
8. Serve immediately.

Creamy Mushroom Soup

Preparation time: 15 minutes
Cooking time: 20 minutes
Total time: 35 minutes
Servings: 4

Nutritional Values:

Calories 271, Total Fat 23.9 g, Saturated Fat 14.6 g,
Cholesterol 70 mg, Sodium 1011 mg, Total Carbs 5.7 g,
Fiber 1 g, Sugar 2.3 g, Protein 9.9 g

Ingredients

- 1 tablespoon butter
- 1 small onion, peeled and chopped
- 1 fresh rosemary sprig
- ½ pound fresh button mushrooms, cleaned and sliced
- 3 cups chicken broth
- ½ teaspoon salt
- 8 ounces cream cheese, softened

How to Prepare

1. In a large-sized soup pan, melt the butter over medium heat and saute the onions and rosemary for about 2-3 minutes.
2. Add in the mushrooms and saute the for about 5-6 minutes.
3. Stir in the broth and salt. Bring it to a boil.
4. Adjust the heat to low and simmer for about 5 minutes.
5. Add in the cream cheese and stir until smooth.
6. Serve hot.

Cheesy Bacon & Cauliflower Soup

Preparation time: 15 minutes
Cooking time: 40 minutes
Total time: 55 minutes
Servings: 6

Nutritional Values:

Calories 339, Total Fat 25.5 g, Saturated Fat 11.9 g,
Cholesterol 71 mg, Sodium 1231 mg, Total Carbs 8.3 g,
Fiber 2.7 g, Sugar 3.5 g, Protein 20 g

Ingredients

- 6 bacon slices
- 3 celery stalks, trimmed and chopped
- 1 small yellow onion, peeled and chopped
- 3 garlic cloves, peeled and minced
- 1½ teaspoons dried thyme
- ¼ teaspoon red pepper flakes
- ½ teaspoon ground black pepper
- 5-6 cups cauliflower, chopped
- 6 cups chicken broth
- 1 cup cheddar cheese, grated
- ¾ cup warm heavy cream
- Salt, as required
- 3-4 tablespoons fresh parsley, chopped

How to Prepare

1. Heat a large-sized soup pan over medium-high heat and cook the bacon for about 8-10 minutes or until crisp.
2. With a slotted spoon, transfer the bacon onto a paper towel-lined plate to drain.
3. Crumble the bacon.
4. In the same pan with bacon grease, add the celery and onions over medium heat and sauté for about 4-5 minutes.
5. Add the garlic, thyme, red pepper flakes, and black pepper. Sauté for about 1 minute.
6. Stir in the cauliflower and broth and bring it to a boil.
7. Adjust the heat to low and simmer for about 20 minutes.
8. Remove from the heat and stir in the cheese, heavy cream, and salt.
9. With an immersion blender, blend the soup until smooth.
10. Serve hot with the garnishing of cooked bacon and parsley.

Spicy Fish Soup

Preparation time: 15 minutes
Cooking time: 35 minutes
Total time: 50 minutes
Servings: 6

Nutritional Values:

Calories 351, Total Fat 11.4 g, Saturated Fat 1.4 g,
Cholesterol 71 mg, Sodium 742 mg, Total Carbs 11.2 g,
Fiber 2.7 g, Sugar 6.3 g, Protein 45.2 g

Ingredients

- 2 pounds snapper fillet, cut into chunks
- 1½ teaspoon ground coriander
- 1 teaspoon ground cumin
- ½ teaspoon ground turmeric
- ½ teaspoon red pepper flakes
- ½ teaspoon paprika
- Salt and ground black pepper, as required
- 3 tablespoons olive oil
- 2 celery stalks, trimmed and chopped
- 1 medium red onion, peeled and chopped
- 1 bell pepper, seeded and chopped
- 4 garlic cloves, peeled and minced
- 1 (28-ounce) can whole peeled tomatoes
- ½ cup white wine
- 5 cups chicken broth
- 2 tablespoons fresh lemon juice
- ¼ cup fresh parsley, chopped

How to Prepare

1. In a bowl, add snapper chunks, spices, salt, and black pepper. Toss to coat well.
2. Transfer the fish chunks onto a plate, reserving the remaining spice mixture.
3. In a large-sized-sized Dutch oven, heat oil over medium-high heat and sauté the celery, onions, bell peppers, and garlic for about 3-4 minutes.
4. Add in the reserved spice mixture and sauté for about 1 minute.
5. Add the tomatoes, wine, and broth. Bring to a full rolling boil.
6. Adjust the heat to medium-low and simmer, partially covered, for about 20 minutes.
7. Add in the fish chunks and cook for about 4-5 minutes.
8. Remove the soup pan from heat and stir in the lemon juice.
9. Serve hot with the garnishing of parsley.

Clam Soup

Preparation time: 15 minutes
Cooking time: 40 minutes
Total time: 55 minutes
Servings: 5

Nutritional Values:

Calories 366, Total Fat 17.8 g, Saturated Fat 7.8 g,
Cholesterol 61 mg, Sodium 275mg, Total Carbs 36.7 g,
Fiber 3.7 g, Sugar 4.2 g, Protein 15.6 g

Ingredients

- 2 tablespoons olive oil
- 1 large onion, peeled and chopped
- 1 celery ribs, trimmed and chopped
- 1 garlic clove, peeled and minced
- 3 small potatoes, peeled and cubed
- 1 (8-ounce) bottle clam juice
- 1 cup water
- 3 teaspoons chicken bouillon granules
- ¼ teaspoon dried thyme, crushed
- ¼ teaspoon ground white pepper
- 1/3 cup all-purpose flour
- 2 cups half-and-half, divided
- 2 (6½-ounce) cans chopped clams, undrained
- 2 tablespoons fresh parsley, chopped

How to Prepare

1. In a large-sized-sized soup pan, heat the oil over medium heat and sauté the onions and celery for about 4-5 minutes.
2. Add the garlic and sauté for about 1 minute.
3. Stir in the potatoes, water, clam juice, bouillon granules, thyme, and white pepper. Bring to a full rolling boil.
4. Adjust the heat to low and simmer, uncovered, for about 15-20 minutes.
5. Meanwhile, in a small-sized bowl, add the flour and 1 cup of half-and-half and mix until smooth.
6. In the pan, slowly add the flour mixture, stirring continuously and bring to a full rolling boil.
7. Cook for about 1-2 minutes, stirring continuously.
8. Stir in the clams and remaining half-and-half and cook for about 2-3 minutes or until heated through, stirring frequently.
9. Serve hot with the topping of parsley.

Beef & Black Bean Soup

Preparation time: 15 minutes
Cooking time: 50 minutes
Total time: 1 hour 5 minutes
Servings: 6

Nutritional Values:

Calories 400, Total Fat 8.4 g, Saturated Fat 2.5 g,
Cholesterol 68 mg, Sodium 680 mg, Total Carbs 43.9 g,
Fiber 14.4 g, Sugar 6.5 g, Protein 38.2 g

Ingredients

- 1-pound lean ground beef
- 1 tablespoon olive oil
- 1 medium onion, peeled and chopped
- 1 carrot, peeled and chopped
- 1 celery stalk, trimmed and chopped
- 1 teaspoon garlic, peeled and minced
- 1 (32-ounce) bottle tomato-vegetable juice cocktail
- 1 (14-ounce) can chicken broth
- 1 teaspoon dried basil
- 1 teaspoon dried parsley
- 1 teaspoon dried oregano
- Ground black pepper, as required
- 2 (15-ounce) cans black beans, drained and rinsed

How to Prepare

1. Heat a large-sized-sized non-stick wok over medium-high heat and cook the beef for about 8-10 minutes, stirring occasionally.
2. Remove the wok from heat and drain the grease.
3. In a large-sized-sized soup pan, heat oil over medium-high heat and sauté the onions, carrots, and celery for about 5 minutes.
4. Add the garlic and sauté for about 1 minute.
5. Stir in the juice cocktail, broth, dried herbs, and black pepper. Bring to a full rolling boil.
6. Adjust the heat to low and simmer for about 20 minutes.
7. Into the soup pan, add cooked beef and beans. Cook for about 10 minutes.
8. Serve hot.

Pork Sausage Soup

Preparation time: 15 minutes
Cooking time: 25 minutes
Total time: 40 minutes
Servings: 5

Nutritional Values:

Calories 306, Total Fat 22.3 g, Saturated 8.7 g, Cholesterol 30 mg, Sodium 964 mg, Total Carbs 8.9 g, Fiber 1.4 g, Sugar 1.7 g, Protein 16.8 g

Ingredients

- 2 tablespoons olive oil
- 12 ounces cooked pork sausage, sliced
- 2 medium celery stalks, trimmed and chopped
- 1 medium onion, peeled and chopped
- 3 large garlic cloves, peeled and crushed
- 2½ cups chicken broth
- 2 ounces cream cheese, softened
- 1 scoop chicken bone broth collagen
- ½ cup heavy whipping cream
- ½ teaspoon salt
- ¼ teaspoon ground black pepper
- 1 tablespoon fresh parsley, minced

How to Prepare

1. In a medium-sized saucepan, heat the oil over medium-high heat and cook the sausage, celery, and onions for about 7 minutes, stirring occasionally.
2. Add the garlic and cook for about 1 minute, stirring continuously.
3. Stir in the broth and bring it to a boil.
4. Adjust the heat to low and simmer, covered, for about 10 minutes
5. Add the cream cheese and bone broth collagen. Stir until well combined and smooth.
6. Stir in the cream, salt, and black pepper. Remove the soup pan from the heat.
7. Garnish with parsley and serve hot.

Turkey & Beans Soup

Preparation time: 15 minutes
Cooking time: 1 hour 10 minutes
Total time: 1 hour 25 minutes
Servings: 8

Nutritional Values:

Calories 404, Total Fat 7.4 g, Saturated Fat 2.4 g,
Cholesterol 87 mg, Sodium 473 mg, Total Carbs 37 g,
Fiber 12 g, Sugar 5.2 g, Protein 46.2 g

Ingredients

- 1 (14½-ounce) can chicken broth
- 1 (15-ounce) can white beans, rinsed and drained
- 2 pounds cooked turkey meat, chopped
- 1 (15-ounce) can black beans, rinsed and drained
- 1 cup fresh corn
- 1 (15-ounce) can diced tomatoes
- ½ large onion, peeled and chopped
- 1 (4-ounce) can chopped green chiles
- 1 jalapeño pepper, seeded and chopped
- 1 garlic clove, peeled and minced
- 1 teaspoon fresh ginger, peeled and minced
- 1 teaspoon dried oregano
- 2 teaspoons citrus seasoning blend
- 1 teaspoon ground cumin
- 1 teaspoon red chili powder
- ½ teaspoon smoked paprika
- ½ teaspoon cayenne pepper
- ½ teaspoon onion powder
- Salt and ground black pepper, as required
- 7 ounces plain Greek yogurt
- 2 tablespoons fresh cilantro, chopped
- 2 tablespoons fresh lime juice

How to Prepare

1. In a large-sized-sized Dutch oven, add the broth and white beans and, with a stick blender, blend until beans are broken down.
2. Add the turkey meat, black beans, corn, tomatoes, onions, green chiles, jalapeño pepper, garlic, ginger, oregano, seasoning blend, and spices. Stir to combine.
3. Place the pan over high heat and bring it to a boil.
4. Adjust the heat to medium-low and simmer, covered, for about 1 hour, stirring frequently.
5. Stir in the salt and black pepper. Remove from the heat.
6. Set aside for about 5 minutes to cool.
7. Add the yogurt, cilantro, and lime juice. Stir to combine well.
8. Serve immediately.

Baked Tomato & Feta Soup

Preparation time: 15 minutes
Cooking time: 1 hour
Total time: 1¼ hours
Servings: 3

Nutritional Values:

*Calories 365, Total Fat 26.8 g, Saturated Fat 8.4 g,
Cholesterol 34 mg, Sodium 911 mg, Total Carbs 22.4 g,
Fiber 3.5 g, Sugar 8.9 g, Protein 12.7 g*

Ingredients

- 4 cups cherry tomatoes
- 2 shallots, peeled and roughly chopped
- 3 garlic cloves, peeled and smashed
- ¼ cup plus 4 teaspoons olive oil, divided
- ¼ teaspoon red pepper flakes
- Salt and ground black pepper, as required
- 4 ounces feta cheese, crumbled
- 2 white bread slices, crusts removed and cut into ½-inch cubes
- 2 cups chicken broth

How to Prepare

1. Preheat your oven to 400 °F.
2. In a medium-sized baking dish, add the tomatoes, shallots, garlic, 1/3 cup of oil, red pepper flakes, salt, and black pepper. Toss to combine.
3. Arrange the tomato mixture in an even layer.
4. Place 2/3 of the feta into the center of the tomato mixture.
5. Drizzle the top of feta with 2 teaspoons of oil.
6. Bake for about 40-45 minutes.
7. Meanwhile, in a small-sized baking dish, add the bread cubes, remaining oil, and ¼ teaspoon of salt. Toss to combine and set aside.
8. Remove the baking dish of tomato mixture from heat.
9. Set the temperature of your oven to 375 °F.
10. Place the baking dish of bread cubes into the oven and bake for about 15 minutes, tossing once halfway through.
11. Meanwhile, in a clean blender, add the tomato mixture and ¼ cup of chicken broth. Pulse until smooth.
12. Transfer the blended mixture into a medium-sized saucepan and stir in the remaining broth.
13. Place the pan of tomato mixture over medium-high heat and bring it to a boil.
14. Adjust the heat to medium-low and cook for about 10 minutes.
15. Serve the soup hot with the topping of croutons.

Lentil & Sweet Potato Soup

Preparation time: 15 minutes
Cooking time: 40 minutes
Total time: 55 minutes
Servings: 6

Nutritional Values:

*Calories 245, Total Fat 4.3 g, Saturated Fat 0.9 g,
Cholesterol 0 mg, Sodium 832 mg, Total Carbs 40.2 g,
Fiber 9.8 g, Sugar 6.1 g, Protein 12.8 g*

Ingredients

- 1 tablespoon vegetable oil
- 4 leeks, peeled and chopped
- 1¾ cups tomatoes, chopped
- 6 cups vegetable broth
- ½ cup brown lentils, rinsed
- 2 sweet potatoes, peeled and cubed
- 4 cups fresh kale, tough ribs removed and chopped
- 1 tablespoon fresh thyme, chopped
- Salt and ground black pepper, as required

How to Prepare

1. In a large-sized-sized soup pan, heat oil over medium heat and sauté leeks for about 3-4 minutes.
2. Add tomatoes and cook for 5-6 minutes, crushing tomatoes with the back of a spoon.
3. Add broth and bring it to a boil.
4. Add lentils, sweet potato, kale, and thyme and again bring to a boil.
5. Adjust the heat to low and simmer, covered, for about 25-30 minutes or until desired doneness.
6. Stir in salt and black pepper. Serve hot.

30-Minute Mushroom & Egg Drop Soup

Preparation time: 15 minutes
Cooking time: 12 minutes
Total time: 27 minutes
Servings: 4

Nutritional Values:

*Calories 129, Total Fat 1.3 g, Saturated Fat 0.2 g,
Cholesterol 0mg, Sodium 46 mg, Total Carbs 31.4 g,
Fiber 5.9 g, Sugar 15.2 g, Protein 1.9 g*

Ingredients

- 8 medium fresh mushrooms, cleaned and sliced thinly
- 4 medium scallions, trimmed and sliced thinly
- 1 teaspoon fresh ginger, peeled and grated
- 4 cups chicken broth
- 4 teaspoons low-sodium soy sauce
- 1 teaspoon ground black pepper
- 4 large eggs
- Salt, as required

How to Prepare

1. In a medium-sized saucepan, add the mushrooms, scallions, ginger, broth, soy sauce, and black pepper over medium-high heat and bring it to a boil.
2. Adjust the heat to low and simmer for about 3-4 minutes.
3. Meanwhile, in a bowl, beat eggs.
4. Slowly, add the beaten eggs in the soup pan, stirring continuously.
5. Simmer for about 1-2 minutes.
6. Stir in salt and serve hot.

30 Minute Smoked Salmon Soup

Preparation time: 10 minutes
Cooking time: 15 minutes
Total time: 25 minutes
Servings: 6

Nutritional Values:

Calories 252, Total Fat 23.1 g, Saturated Fat 13.9 g, Cholesterol 79 mg, Sodium 1011 mg, Total Carbs 2.9 g, Fiber 0.4 g, Sugar 0.8 g, Protein 8.8 g

Ingredients

- 2 tablespoons salted butter
- 1 celery stalk, trimmed and chopped
- ¼ cup onion, peeled and chopped
- ½ teaspoon salt
- 1 garlic clove, peeled and minced
- 1½ cups chicken broth
- 1 tablespoon tomato paste
- 4 ounces cream cheese
- 6 ounces smoked salmon, chopped
- 1½ cups heavy whipping cream
- 2 tablespoons capers

How to Prepare

1. In a large-sized saucepan, melt the butter over medium heat and sauté the celery, onions, and salt for about 5 minutes.
2. Add the garlic and sauté for about 1 minute.
3. Stir in the broth and tomato paste and bring to a simmer.
4. Remove from the heat and set aside to cool slightly.
5. Into a blender, add the cream cheese and broth mixture. Pulse until smooth.
6. Return to the pan over medium-low heat and stir in the salmon, cream, and capers.
7. Cook for about 3-5 minutes, stirring frequently.
8. Serve hot.

Lasagna & Sausage Soup

Preparation time: 15 minutes
Cooking time: 40 minutes
Total time: 55 minutes
Servings: 8

Nutritional Values:

*Calories 483, Total Fat 27.9 g, Saturated Fat 10.7 g,
Cholesterol 70 mg, Sodium 1311 mg, Total Carbs 35.4 g,
Fiber 2.4 g, Sugar 14.3 g, Protein 25.9 g*

Ingredients

- 16 ounces mild ground Italian sausage
- 2 tablespoons olive oil
- 1½ cups white onion, peeled and chopped
- 4 garlic cloves, peeled and minced
- 8 uncooked lasagna noodles, broken into 1x1-inch pieces
- 1 (23¼-ounce) can tomato soup
- 1 (14½-ounce) can petite diced tomatoes
- 1 (12-ounce) can evaporated milk
- 2 teaspoons dried basil
- 2 teaspoons paprika
- Salt and ground black pepper, as required
- 8 ounces mozzarella cheese, shredded
- ¼ cup fresh parsley, chopped

How to Prepare

1. Heat a Dutch oven on over medium-high heat and cook the sausage for about 4-5 minutes, stirring frequently.
2. With a slotted spoon, transfer the sausage into a bowl and drain the grease from the Dutch oven.
3. In the Dutch oven, heat the oil over medium heat and sauté the onions and garlic for about 4-5 minutes.
4. Stir in the cooked sausage, lasagna noodles, tomato soup, tomatoes, evaporated milk, basil, paprika, salt, and black pepper. Bring to a boil, stirring occasionally.
5. Boil for about 3 minutes, stirring frequently.
6. Adjust the heat to medium-low and simmer for about 25 minutes, stirring occasionally.
7. Serve hot with the topping of mozzarella and parsley.

Pasta & Meatballs Soup

Preparation time: 20 minutes
Cooking time: 40 minutes
Total time: 1 hour
Servings: 6

Nutritional Values:

*Calories 360, Total Fat 15.8 g, Saturated Fat 4.6 g,
Cholesterol 102 mg, Sodium 1245 mg, Total Carbs 24.2 g,
Fiber 2.6 g, Sugar 4.2 g, Protein 30.3 g*

Ingredients

- 16 ounces mild ground Italian sausage
- 2 tablespoons olive oil
- 1½ cups white onion, peeled and chopped
- 4 garlic cloves, peeled and minced
- 8 uncooked lasagna noodles, broken into 1x1-inch pieces
- 1 (23¼-ounce) can tomato soup
- 1 (14½-ounce) can petite diced tomatoes
- 1 (12-ounce) can evaporated milk
- 2 teaspoons dried basil
- 2 teaspoons paprika
- Salt and ground black pepper, as required
- 8 ounces mozzarella cheese, shredded
- ¼ cup fresh parsley, chopped

How to Prepare

1. For meatballs: in a large-sized-sized bowl, add all ingredients, except for oil, and mix until well combined.
2. Make equal-sized small balls from mixture.
3. In a large-sized-sized non-stick wok, heat oil over medium-high heat and cook the meatballs in 2 batches for about 4 minutes or until browned, flipping occasionally.
4. With a slotted spoon, transfer the meatballs onto a paper towel-lined plate.
5. For soup: in a large-sized-sized soup pan, heat oil over medium-high heat and cook the onions, carrots, and celery for about 6-8 minutes, stirring frequently.
6. Add in garlic and saute for about 1 minute.
7. Add in broth, salt, and black pepper. Bring to a full rolling boil.
8. Add in pasta and meatballs and again bring to a gentle boil.
9. Adjust the heat to medium-low and cook, covered for about 10 minutes, stirring occasionally.
10. Add in spinach and cook for about 2-3 minutes.
11. Serve hot.

This page is for your notes

This page is for your notes

This page is for your notes

This page is for your notes

This page is for your notes

Winter Soups

Classic Chicken Enchilada Soup

Preparation time: 15 minutes
Cooking time: 50 minutes
Total time: 1 hour 5 minutes
Servings: 8

Nutritional Values:

Calories 429, Total Fat 19.8 g, Saturated Fat 6.9 g,
Cholesterol 115 mg, Sodium 724 mg, Total Carbs 30.6 g,
Fiber 11.1 g, Sugar 3.9 g, Protein 43.6 g

Ingredients

Soup
- 2 tablespoons olive oil
- 2 pounds boneless, skinless chicken breasts
- 1 medium onion, peeled and chopped
- 2 poblano peppers, chopped finely
- 3 garlic cloves, peeled and minced
- 1 (14½-ounce) can diced tomatoes with juice
- 1 (10-ounce) can enchilada sauce
- 2 tablespoons tomato paste
- ½-1 teaspoon chipotle hot pepper sauce
- 1 tablespoon red chili powder
- 2 teaspoons ground cumin
- ½ teaspoon ground black pepper
- 48 ounces canned chicken broth

Topping
- ½ cup sour cream
- ½ cup cheddar cheese, shredded
- ½ cup fresh cilantro, chopped

How to Prepare

1. In a large-sized soup pan, heat the oil over medium heat and cook the chicken breasts for about 4-5 minutes.
2. With a slotted spoon, transfer the chicken breasts into a bowl.
3. In the pan, add the onions and poblano peppers for about 3-4 minutes, stirring frequently.
4. Add the garlic and sauté for about 1 minute.
5. Add the cooked chicken and remaining ingredients. Stir to combine.
6. Adjust the heat to high and bring it to a boil.
7. Adjust the heat to low and cook, covered, for about 25-30 minutes.
8. Uncover the pan and with a slotted spoon, transfer the chicken breasts into a bowl.
9. With 2 forks, shred the meat.
10. Return the shredded meat into the pan and cook for about 4-5 minutes.
11. Serve hot with the topping of sour cream, cheddar cheese, and cilantro.

Classic Zuppa Toscana

Preparation time: 15 minutes
Cooking time: 40 minutes
Total time: 55 minutes
Servings: 6

Nutritional Values:

Calories 362, Total Fat 29.4 g, Saturated Fat 11.6 g,
Cholesterol 91 mg, Sodium 899 mg, Total Carbs 6.2 g,
Fiber 1.9 g, Sugar 2.3 g, Protein 18.1 g

Ingredients

- 1-pound mild Italian sausage
- 1 onion, peeled and chopped
- 3 garlic cloves, peeled and minced
- 1 head cauliflower, cut into florets
- 16 ounces chicken broth
- 4 cups water
- ½ teaspoon red pepper flakes
- Salt and ground black pepper, as required
- 3 cups fresh Swiss chard, chopped
- 1 cup heavy cream

How to Prepare

1. Heat a large-sized soup pan over medium-high heat and cook the sausage for about 6-8 minutes or until browned, crumbling with a wooden spoon.
2. Add the onions and garlic and cook for about 4-5 minutes.
3. Stir in the cauliflower, broth, water, red pepper flakes, salt, and black pepper Bring to a boil.
4. Adjust the heat to medium and cook for about 15-20 minutes.
5. Add the Swiss chard and stir to combine.
6. Adjust the heat to low and cook for about 2-3 minutes.
7. Add in the cream and cook for about 2-3 minutes, stirring continuously.
8. Serve hot.

Classic Ham & Beans Soup

Preparation time: 15 minutes
Cooking time: 2 hours
Total time: 2¼ hours
Servings: 8

Nutritional Values:

Calories 403, Total Fat 12.4 g, Saturated Fat 3.8 g,
Cholesterol 65 mg, Sodium 1211 mg, Total Carbs 41 g,
Fiber 107 g, Sugar 2.3 g, Protein 32.4 g

Ingredients

- 1-pound dry white beans
- 2-3 pounds smoked ham shanks
- 8 cups water
- 2 teaspoons Italian seasoning
- 1 tablespoon extra-virgin olive oil
- 1 small onion, peeled and chopped
- 2 garlic cloves, peeled and minced
- 1 cup celery, trimmed and chopped
- 2/3 cup carrots, peeled and chopped
- 3-4 drops Tabasco sauce
- Salt and ground black pepper, as required

How to Prepare

1. In a large-sized-sized soup pan of water, add the beans over high heat and bring to a full rolling boil.
2. Remove the soup pan from heat and soak the beans for about 2 hours.
3. Drain the water completely.
4. In a Dutch oven, add ham shanks, water, and Italian seasoning over high heat. Bring to a full rolling boil.
5. Adjust the heat to low and simmer, partially covered, for about 1 hour.
6. Meanwhile, in a small-sized wok, heat oil over medium-high heat and sauté the onions for about 5-6 minutes.
7. Add the garlic and sauté for about 1 minute.
8. Remove the soup pan from heat and transfer the onion mixture in the pan with ham.
9. Stir in the drained beans, celery, and carrot. Cook uncovered for about 45 minutes.
10. With a slotted spoon, transfer the ham bones into a bowl.
11. Pull off any meat from the bones and return into the soup.
12. Discard the bones.
13. In the soup, stir in the Tabasco sauce, salt, and black pepper. Remove the soup pan from heat.
14. Serve hot.

Classic Jambalaya Soup

Preparation time: 20 minutes
Cooking time: 30 minutes
Total time: 50 minutes
Servings: 6

Nutritional Values:

Calories 258, Total Fat 11.2 g, Saturated Fat 3.3 g,
Cholesterol 155 mg, Sodium 1121 mg, Total Carbs 9.2 g,
Fiber 2 g, Sugar 4.1 g, Protein 29.9 g

Ingredients

- 1 tablespoon olive oil
- 1 cup onion, peeled and chopped
- 1 cup bell peppers, seeded and chopped
- 2 celery stalks, trimmed and chopped
- 6 ounces okra
- ¾ cup tomatoes, chopped
- 1 teaspoon garlic, peeled and crushed
- 2 bay leaves
- 2 tablespoons Cajun seasoning
- Salt and ground black pepper, as required
- 6 cups chicken broth
- 6 ounces kielbasa sausage, chopped
- 12 ounces shrimp
- 1 cup cooked chicken, chopped
- ¼ cup fresh parsley, chopped

How to Prepare

1. In a large-sized soup pan, heat the olive oil over medium heat and sauté the onions, bell pepper, and celery for about 4-5 minutes.
2. Stir in the okra, tomatoes, garlic, bay leaves, Cajun seasoning, salt, black pepper, and broth. Bring it to a boil.
3. Cook for about 5-6 minutes.
4. Add kielbasa pieces and cook for about 10 minutes.
5. Stir in the shrimp and chicken. Cook for about 5 minutes.
6. Serve hot with the garnishing of parsley.

Creamy Chicken Gnocchi Soup

Preparation time: 15 minutes
Cooking time: 15 minutes
Total time: 30 minutes
Servings: 8

Nutritional Values:

*Calories 380, Total Fat 23.1 g, Saturated Fat 12.9 g,
Cholesterol 74 mg, Sodium 784 mg, Total Carbs 29.4 g,
Fiber 2.5 g, Sugar 1.9 g, Protein 13.6 g*

Ingredients

- 4 tablespoons butter
- 1 tablespoon extra virgin olive oil
- 1 cup onion, peeled and chopped finely
- ½ cup celery, trimmed and chopped finely
- 2 garlic cloves, peeled and minced
- ¼ cup all-purpose flour
- 4 cups half-and-half
- 28 ounces chicken broth
- 1 (16-ounce) package ready-to-use gnocchi
- 1 cup cooked chicken breast, chopped
- 1 cup fresh spinach leaves, chopped
- 1 cup carrots, peeled and shredded finely
- ½ teaspoon dried parsley flakes
- ½ teaspoon dried thyme
- ¼ teaspoon ground nutmeg
- Salt, as required

How to Prepare

1. In a large-sized soup pan, melt the butter with oil over medium heat and cook the onions, celery, and garlic for about 5-6 minutes, stirring occasionally.
2. Stir in the flour and cook for about 1 minute.
3. Add the half-and-half and beat until well combined.
4. Simmer until thickened, stirring continuously.
5. Stir in the broth and simmer until thickened.
6. Stir in gnocchi, chicken, spinach, carrots, dried herbs, nutmeg, and salt. Cook for about 3-5 minutes, stirring occasionally.
7. Serve hot.

Cheese Soup

Preparation time: 15 minutes
Cooking time: 1 hour 5 minutes
Total time: 1 hour 20 minutes
Servings: 4

Nutritional Values:

Calories 269, Total Fat 19.9 g, Saturated Fat 12 g,
Cholesterol 53 mg, Sodium 1011 mg, Total Carbs 15.6 g,
Fiber 1.4 g, Sugar 8.4 g, Protein 8.1 g

Ingredients

Soup
- 2 tablespoons unsalted butter
- 2 cups yellow onions, peeled and sliced thinly
- 14½ ounces canned chicken broth
- Salt and ground black pepper, as required
- 2 chicken bouillon cubes
- ¼ cup Velveeta cheese

White Sauce
- 3 tablespoons butter
- 3 tablespoons all-purpose flour
- ¼ teaspoon salt
- 1½ cups whole milk

How to Prepare

1. For soup: in a large-sized soup pan, place butter and onions over medium-low heat and cook for about 8-10 minutes, stirring frequently.
2. Add broth, bouillon cubes, salt, and black pepper. Cook for about 3-4 minutes.
3. Meanwhile, for white sauce: in a large-sized pan, melt butter over medium heat.
4. Add the flour and cook until thickened, stirring continuously.
5. Slowly add milk, beating continuously until smooth and thick.
6. Stir in salt and remove from heat.
7. In the pan of soup, add white sauce and Velveeta cheese and stir to combine.
8. Adjust the heat to medium-low and cook for about 2-3 minutes, stirring continuously.
9. Adjust the heat to low and simmer for about 30-45 minutes.
10. Serve hot.

Cheesy Bacon & Jalapeño Soup

Preparation time: 15 minutes
Cooking time: 35 minutes
Total time: 50 minutes
Servings: 5

Nutritional Values:

*Calories 586, Total Fat 51.4 g, Saturated Fat 26.3 g,
Cholesterol 145 mg, Sodium 1921 mg, Total Carbs 3.4 g,
Fiber 0.6 g, Sugar 1.4 g, Protein 28 g*

Ingredients

- ½ pound bacon slices, chopped
- 4 medium jalapeño peppers, chopped
- 3 cups chicken broth
- 4 tablespoons butter
- 1 teaspoon dried thyme
- 1 teaspoon onion powder
- 1 teaspoon garlic powder
- ½ teaspoon ground cumin
- ½ teaspoon celery seed
- 8 ounces cheddar cheese, shredded
- ¾ cup heavy cream
- Salt and ground black pepper, as required

How to Prepare

1. Heat a large-sized soup pan over medium-high heat and cook the bacon for about 8-10 minutes or until crisp.
2. With a slotted spoon, transfer the bacon onto a paper towel-lined plate to drain.
3. Crumble the bacon.
4. In the same pan with bacon grease, add the jalapeño peppers and sauté for about 1-2 minutes.
5. With a slotted spoon, transfer the jalapeño peppers into a bowl.
6. In the same pan, add the broth, butter, thyme, and spices. Bring to a boil.
7. Adjust the heat to low and simmer for about 15 minutes.
8. Remove from the heat and stir in the cheese, heavy cream, salt, and black pepper.
9. With an immersion blender, blend the soup until smooth.
10. Return the soup over medium heat and stir in the cooked bacon and jalapeño peppers.
11. Simmer for about 5 minutes, stirring frequently.
12. Serve hot.

Halibut & Quinoa Soup

Preparation time: 15 minutes
Cooking time: 1 hour 10 minutes
Total time: 1 hour 25 minutes
Servings: 6

Nutritional Values:

Calories 362, Total Fat 14.7 g, Saturated Fat 9.2 g,
Cholesterol 24 mg, Sodium 8901 mg, Total Carbs 30.8 g,
Fiber 5.5 g, Sugar 5 g, Protein 27.9 g

Ingredients

- 2 cups onions, peeled and chopped
- 1 cup celery, trimmed and chopped
- 2 garlic cloves, peeled and chopped
- 2 tablespoons fresh ginger root, finely chopped
- 1 cup fresh shiitake mushrooms, cleaned and sliced
- 1 cup quinoa, rinsed
- 6-7 cups chicken broth
- 16 ounces halibut fillets
- 8 cups fresh baby spinach
- 1 cup fresh cilantro, chopped
- 1 cup unsweetened coconut milk
- Salt, as required

How to Prepare

1. Into a large-sized-sized soup pan, place onions, celery, garlic, ginger, mushrooms, quinoa, and broth over high heat. Cook until boiling.
2. Adjust the heat to low and cook, covered, for about 45 minutes.
3. Arrange the halibut fillets over soup mixture.
4. Cook, covered for about 15 minutes.
5. Stir in the remaining ingredients and simmer for about 5 minutes.
6. Serve hot.

Shrimp Soup

Preparation time: 15 minutes
Cooking time: 15 minutes
Total time: 30 minutes
Servings: 6

Nutritional Values:

Calories 297, Total Fat 17.7 g, Saturated Fat 10.1 g,
Cholesterol 290 mg, Sodium 724 mg, Total Carbs 4.3 g,
Fiber 0.6 g, Sugar 0.7 g, Protein 29.1 g

Ingredients

- 2 tablespoons butter
- ¼ cup onion, peeled and chopped finely
- 3 cups chicken broth
- 1½ cups heavy whipping cream
- 2 teaspoons smoked paprika
- Salt, as required
- 2 teaspoons ground black pepper
- 1½ pounds shrimp, peeled, deveined, and roughly chopped

How to Prepare

1. In a large-sized soup pan, melt butter over medium heat and cook the onions for about 4-5 minutes.
2. Add the broth, heavy whipping cream, paprika, salt, and black pepper. Bring it to a boil.
3. Stir in shrimp and simmer for about 4-5 minutes, stirring frequently.
4. Serve hot.

Beef & Barley Soup

Preparation time: 15 minutes
Cooking time: 35 minutes
Total time: 50 minutes
Servings: 4

Nutritional Values:

*Calories 277, Total Fat 10.1 g, Saturated Fat 2.5 g,
Cholesterol 51 mg, Sodium 829 mg, Total Carbs 21.7 g,
Fiber 3.6 g, Sugar 4 g, Protein 25 g*

Ingredients

- 8 ounces sirloin steak, trimmed and cut into bite-sized pieces
- Salt and ground pepper, as required
- 4 teaspoons extra-virgin olive oil, divided
- 1 large carrot, peeled and chopped
- 1 large celery stalk, trimmes and sliced
- 1 medium onion, peeled and chopped
- 2 tablespoons tomato paste
- 1 tablespoon fresh thyme, chopped
- ¾ cup quick-cooking barley
- 4 cups beef broth
- 1 cup water
- 2 teaspoons fresh lemon juice

How to Prepare

1. Sprinkle the steak pieces evenly with salt and black pepper.
2. In a Dutch oven, heat 2 teaspoons of oil over medium heat and sear steak for about 2-3 minutes.
3. Transfer the steak into a bowl.
4. In the same soup pan, heat the remaining oil over medium heat and sauté carrots, celery, and onions for about 4-5 minutes.
5. Add tomato paste and thyme. Cook for about 1-2 minutes.
6. Add cooked beef, barley, broth, water, salt, and black pepper. Bring to a full rolling boil.
7. Adjust the heat to low and simmer for about 15-20 minutes.
8. Stir in lemon juice and serve hot.

Pork & Vegetable Soup

Preparation time: 15 minutes
Cooking time: 2 hours
Total time: 2¼ hours
Servings: 6

Nutritional Values:

Calories 462, Total Fat 13.1 g, Saturated Fat 3.5 g,
Cholesterol 65 mg, Sodium 502 mg, Total Carbs 45 g,
Fiber 7.3 g, Sugar 7.4 g, Protein 30.4 g

Ingredients

- 1 pound pork stew meat, cut into cubes
- Salt and ground black pepper, as required
- 3 carrots, peeled and chopped
- 2 celery stalks, trimmed and chopped
- 2 tablespoons olive oil, divided
- 1 medium onion, peeled and chopped
- 3 garlic cloves, peeled and minced
- 4 tablespoons all-purpose flour
- 3 cups beef broth
- 2 tablespoons tomato paste
- 1 teaspoon dried thyme
- 2 bay leaves
- 1½ cups dry red wine
- 1½ cups water
- 3 large potatoes, cut into cubes
- 1 cup frozen green peas

How to Prepare

1. Sprinkle the pork cubes with salt and black pepper evenly.
2. In a large-sized-sized heavy-bottomed soup pan, heat 1 tablespoon of oil over high heat and sear the pork cubes for about 4-5 minutes or until browned on all sides.
3. With a slotted spoon, transfer the pork cubes into a bowl.
4. In the same soup pan, heat the remaining oil over medium heat and sauté the carrots, celery, onions, and garlic for about 3-4 minutes.
5. Add the flour and stir to combine.
6. Slowly add in the broth, stirring continuously until well combined.
7. Stir in cooked beef, tomato paste, thyme, bay leaves, wine, and water. Bring to a full rolling boil.
8. Adjust the heat to low and simmer, covered, for about 1¼ hours.
9. Stir in the potatoes and peas. Simmer for about 20-30 minutes.
10. Stir in salt and black pepper. Serve hot.

Chicken & Salsa Soup

Preparation time: 15 minutes
Cooking time: 20 minutes
Total time: 35 minutes
Servings: 6

Nutritional Values:

Calories 539, Total Fat 34.7 g, Saturated Fat 26.4 g,
Cholesterol 209 mg, Sodium 1011 mg, Total Carbs 11.8 g,
Fiber 1.6 g, Sugar 1.9 g, Protein 45 g

Ingredients

- 2 pounds boneless, skinless chicken thighs
- 24 ounces chicken broth
- 1 (28-ounce) can green enchilada sauce
- 4 ounces green salsa
- 2 cups Monterey Jack cheese, shredded
- 1 cup heavy cream
- 4 ounces cream cheese, cubed
- Salt and ground black pepper, as required

How to Prepare

1. In a large-sized-sized soup pan, add chicken and broth over medium heat and cook for about 10-15 minutes.
2. With a slotted spoon, transfer the chicken thighs onto a plate.
3. Chop the chicken thighs into bite-sized pieces.
4. Into the pan with broth, add the chopped chicken and remaining ingredients and cook for about 5 minutes.
5. Serve hot.

French Onion Soup

Preparation time: 15 minutes
Cooking time: 50 minutes
Total time: 1 hour 5 minutes
Servings: 4

Nutritional Values:

Calories 358, Total Fat 21.2 g, Saturated Fat 10.2 g,
Cholesterol 45 mg, Sodium 934 mg, Total Carbs 23.5 g,
Fiber 2.8 g, Sugar 5.8 g, Protein 12.9 g

Ingredients

- 4 tablespoons butter
- 3 large white onions, peeled and thinly sliced
- 2 tablespoons all-purpose flour
- ½ cup white wine
- Salt and ground black pepper, as required
- 8 fresh thyme sprigs
- 2 cups chicken broth
- 2 cups beef broth
- 4 baguette slices
- ½ cup Gruyere cheese, grated

How to Prepare

1. Melt butter in a large-sized-sized soup pan over medium-high heat and cook onions for about 25 minutes, stirring occasionally.
2. Add flour and immediately stir to combine.
3. Cook for about 1 minute, stirring continuously.
4. Stir in wine, salt, and black pepper. Simmer for about 2-3 minutes.
5. Add thyme sprigs, and chicken and beef broths, and bring it to a boil.
6. Adjust the heat to medium and simmer for about 15 minutes.
7. Preheat the broiler of the oven to high.
8. Remove the soup pan from heat and discard the thyme sprigs.
9. Place baguette slices on a large-sized baking sheet and top each slice with 2 tablespoons of cheese.
10. Transfer the baking sheet into oven and broil for about 1 minute or until cheese is bubbling and golden brown.
10. Transfer soup into bowls and serve with the topping of the bread slices.

Potato & Corn Soup

Preparation time: 15 minutes
Cooking time: 25 minutes
Total time: 40 minutes
Servings: 4

Nutritional Values:

*Calories 326, Total Fat 17.1 g, Saturated Fat 9.9 g,
Cholesterol 49 mg, Sodium 689 mg, Total Carbs 37.1 g,
Fiber 5.7 g, Sugar 6 g, Protein 9.2 g*

Ingredients

- 2 tablespoons unsalted butter
- 2 celery stalks, trimmed and chopped
- 1 large onion, peeled and chopped
- 2 garlic cloves, peeled and minced
- 2 medium baking potatoes, peeled and chopped
- ½ teaspoon dried thyme
- 1 bay leaf
- Salt and ground black pepper, as required
- 3 cups chicken broth
- 2 cups frozen corn
- 1 cup light cream

How to Prepare

1. In a large-sized-sized soup pan, melt butter over medium heat and sauté celery, onions, and garlic for about 4-6 minutes.
2. Add potatoes, thyme, bay leaf, salt, black pepper, and broth. Bring it to a boil.
3. Adjust the heat to low and simmer, covered, for about 8-10 minutes.
4. Stir in corn and cream. Simmer for about 4 minutes.
5. Remove the soup pan from heat and discard the bay leaf.
6. With a potato masher, mash some of the potatoes slightly.
7. Serve immediately.

30 Minute Egg Drop Soup

Preparation time: 10 minutes
Cooking time: 10 minutes
Total time: 20 minutes
Servings: 4

Nutritional Values:

*Calories 142, Total Fat 11.1 g, Saturated Fat 2.2 g,
Cholesterol 93 mg, Sodium 874 mg, Total Carbs 2.5 g,
Fiber 0.4 g, Sugar 1.2 g, Protein 8.4 g*

Ingredients

- 2 tablespoons olive oil
- 1 teaspoon fresh ginger root, peeled and chopped finely
- 1 garlic clove, peeled and chopped finely
- ½ teaspoon sesame seeds
- 4 cups chicken broth
- 2 large eggs
- 1/8 teaspoon salt
- ¼ teaspoon ground black pepper
- ½ cup scallion, trimmed and chopped

How to Prepare

1. In a soup pan, heat the oil over medium heat and sauté the ginger, garlic, and sesame seeds for about 1 minute.
2. Add the broth and stir to combine.
3. Cover the pan and bring to a simmer.
4. Meanwhile, in a bowl, beat together the egg, salt, and black pepper.
5. Slowly add the beaten eggs in the pan, stirring continuously.
6. Stir in the scallions and simmer, uncovered, for about 5 minutes.
7. Serve hot.

30-Minute Tofu & Mushroom Soup

Preparation time: 15 minutes
Cooking time: 15 minutes
Total time: 30 minutes
Servings: 2

Nutritional Values:

Calories 137, Total Fat 5 g, Saturated Fat 14 g, Cholesterol 0 mg, Sodium 911 mg, Total Carbs 10.8 g, Fiber 1.5 g, Sugar 4 g, Protein 13.5 g

Ingredients

- 3 cups vegetable broth
- ½ cup fresh shiitake mushrooms, cleaned and sliced
- 1 tablespoon low-sodium soy sauce
- 1 tablespoon miso paste
- ½ cup soft tofu, cubed
- 1 scallion, trimmed and chopped

How to Prepare

1. In a medium-sized saucepan, add the broth over medium-high heat and bring it to a boil.
2. Add the mushrooms and stir to combine.
3. Adjust the heat to medium-low and simmer for about 4-5 minutes.
4. Meanwhile, in a small-sized bowl, mix together the soy sauce and miso paste.
5. Into the pan of soup, add the tofu and miso mixture. Simmer for about 5 minutes.
6. Stir in the scallions and serve.

Pasta & Bean Soup

Preparation time: 15 minutes
Cooking time: 35 minutes
Total time: 50 minutes
Servings: 6

Nutritional Values:

Calories 346, Total Fat 4.3 g, Saturated Fat 1 g,
Cholesterol 12 mg, Sodium 811 mg, Total Carbs 60.8 g,
Fiber 13 g, Sugar 9.5 g, Protein 17.9 g

Ingredients

- 2 teaspoons vegetable oil
- 1 large leek, cleaned and chopped
- 1 large carrot, trimmed, peeled, and chopped
- 4 garlic cloves, peeled and minced
- 1 teaspoon dried rosemary, crushed
- 1 teaspoon red pepper flakes
- 1/8 teaspoon paprika
- 2 large potatoes, peeled and chopped
- 6 cups vegetable broth
- 2 (15-ounce) cans red kidney beans, rinsed and drained
- 1 (28-ounce) can diced tomatoes
- 1 cup pasta (your choice)
- Salt and ground black pepper, as required

How to Prepare

1. In a large-sized-sized soup pan, heat oil over medium heat and sauté leeks, carrots, garlic, rosemary, and spices for about 3 minutes.
2. Add broth and potatoes. Bring to a full rolling boil.
3. Boil for about 1-2 minutes.
4. Adjust the heat to low and cook, covered, for about 15 minutes.
5. Stir in beans, tomatoes, and pasta. Cook for about 10 minutes.
6. Stir in salt and black pepper. and serve hot.

Pasta & Sausage Soup

Preparation time: 15 minutes
Cooking time: 25 minutes
Total time: 40 minutes
Servings: 6

Nutritional Values:

Calories 346, Total Fat 4.3 g, Saturated Fat 1 g,
Cholesterol 12 mg, Sodium 811 mg, Total Carbs 60.8 g,
Fiber 13 g, Sugar 9.5 g, Protein 17.9 g

Ingredients

- 2 tablespoons extra-virgin olive oil
- 1-pound spicy Italian sausage, sliced
- 1 medium yellow onion, peeled and finely chopped
- 2 medium carrots, peeled and finely chopped
- 2 celery stalks, trimmed and finely chopped
- 3 garlic cloves, peeled and minced
- Salt and ground black pepper, as required
- 2 (15-ounce) cans Great Northern Beans, with liquid
- 1 (15-ounce) can diced tomatoes
- 4 cups chicken broth
- 2 fresh rosemary sprigs, finely chopped
- 1½ cups pasta (your choice)

How to Prepare

1. In a large-sized, heavy-bottomed pan, heat oil over medium heat and cook the sausage about 5 minutes, stirring frequently.
2. Stir in onions, carrots, and celery. Cook for about 5 minutes.
3. Add garlic, salt, and pepper. Cook for about 1 minute.
4. Add in the beans with liquid, tomatoes, broth, and rosemary. Bring it to a boil.
5. Add in pasta and stir to combine.
6. Adjust the heat to medium and cook for about 8 minutes.
7. Serve hot.

This page is for your notes

This page is for your notes

This page is for your notes

This page is for your notes

This page is for your notes

Stew Recipes

Chicken & Spinach Stew

Preparation time: 15 minutes
Cooking time: 35 minutes
Total time: 50 minutes
Servings: 4

Nutritional Values:

Calories 374, Total Fat 26.5 g, Saturated Fat 7.8 g,
Cholesterol 95 mg, Sodium 170 mg, Total Carbs 11.7 g,
Fiber 3.9 g, Sugar 2.9 g, Protein 23.2 g

Ingredients

- 2 tablespoons olive oil
- 1 medium onion, peeled and chopped
- 1 tablespoon garlic, peeled and minced
- 1 tablespoon fresh ginger root, peeled and minced
- 1 teaspoon ground turmeric
- 1 teaspoon ground cumin
- 1 teaspoon ground coriander
- 1 teaspoon paprika
- 4 (4-ounce) boneless, skinless chicken thighs, cut into 1-inch pieces
- 4 tomatoes, chopped
- 14 ounces unsweetened coconut milk
- Salt and ground black pepper, as required
- 6 cups fresh spinach, chopped
- 2 tablespoons fresh lemon juice

How to Prepare

1. Heat oil in a large-sized-sized heavy-bottomed pan over medium heat and sauté the onions for about 3-4 minutes.
2. Add the ginger, garlic, and spices. Sauté for about 1 minute.
3. Add the chicken and cook for about 4-5 minutes.
4. Add the tomatoes, coconut milk, salt, and black pepper. Cook until boiling.
5. Adjust the heat to low and cook, covered, for about 10-15 minutes.
6. Add in the spinach and cook for about 4-5 minutes.
7. Add in lemon juice and remove from heat.
8. Serve hot.

Chicken & Vegetable Stew

Preparation time: 15 minutes
Cooking time: 35 minutes
Total time: 50 minutes
Servings: 6

Nutritional Values:

Calories 365, Total Fat 19.5 g, Saturated Fat 8.8 g,
Cholesterol 131 mg, Sodium 653 mg, Total Carbs 8.3 g,
Fiber 2.9 g, Sugar 3.6 g, Protein 39.3 g

Ingredients

- 3 tablespoons unsalted butter
- ½ cup yellow onion, peeled and chopped
- ¾ cup bell pepper, seeded and chopped
- 3¾ cups chicken broth
- 1 bay leaf
- 2/3 cup fluid whipping cream
- 12 ounces asparagus, ends trimmed and cut into 2-inch pieces
- 8 ounces fresh mushrooms, cleaned and sliced
- 1 cup fresh green beans, washed and cut into 2-inch pieces
- 1½ pounds cooked boneless chicken, chopped
- Salt and ground black pepper, as required
- 2 tablespoons fresh thyme, minced

How to Prepare

1. In a large-sized pan, melt the butter over medium heat and sauté the onions and bell pepper for about 4-5 minutes.
2. Add the broth and bay leaf. Bring it to a boil.
3. Cook for about 10 minutes.
4. Meanwhile, in a small-sized pan, add cream over medium heat and cook for about 5-7 minutes, stirring occasionally.
5. Add the asparagus, mushrooms, and green beans into the pan of broth mixture and cook for about 7-10 minutes.
6. Add the cooked chicken and stir to combine.
7. Adjust the heat to low and simmer for about 3-5 minutes.
8. Stir in the salt, black pepper, thyme and cream. Immediately remove from the heat.
9. Serve hot.

Chicken & Chickpeas Stew

Preparation time: 15 minutes
Cooking time: 1¼ hours
Total time: 1½ hours
Servings: 8

Nutritional Values:

Calories 348, Total Fat 13 g, Saturated Fat 2.4 g,
Cholesterol 95 mg, Sodium 778 mg, Total Carbs 28.5 g,
Fiber 5.7 g, Sugar 3.3 g, Protein 30.1 g

Ingredients

- 8 (4-ounce) skinless, boneless chicken thighs
- Salt and ground black pepper, as required
- ¼ cup extra-virgin olive oil
- 3 large yellow onions, peeled and sliced thinly
- 8 garlic cloves, peeled and crushed
- 3 small red chiles, stemmed
- 2 fresh bay leaves
- 1 tablespoon ground turmeric
- 2 teaspoons ground coriander
- 2 teaspoons ground cumin
- 2 (2-inch) cinnamon sticks
- 4 teaspoons fresh lemon zest, grated
- ½ cup fresh lemon juice, divided
- 4 cups chicken broth
- 3 cups canned chickpeas, rinsed and drained
- ½ cup fresh cilantro, chopped

How to Prepare

1. Rub the chicken thighs with salt and black pepper evenly.
2. In a large-sized-sized Dutch oven, heat the oil over medium-high heat.
3. Add the chicken thighs in 2 batches and cook for about 3-4 minutes per side.
4. With a slotted spoon, transfer the chicken thighs into a bowl.
5. In the same pan, add the onions over medium heat and sauté for about 3-4 minutes.
6. Add the garlic, red chiles, bay leaves, and spices. Sauté for about 1 minute.
7. Add the cooked chicken, lemon zest, 1/3 cup of the lemon juice, and broth. Bring it to a boil.
8. Adjust the heat to medium-low and simmer, covered, for about 15 minutes.
9. Add the cooked chicken and cook for about 15 minutes.
10. Add the olives and chickpeas. Stir to combine.
11. Adjust the heat to medium-high and cook for about 6-8 minutes, stirring occasionally.
12. Stir in the remaining lemon juice, salt, and black pepper. Remove from heat.
13. Discard the cinnamon sticks and serve hot with the garnishing of cilantro.

Turkey & Pasta Stew

Preparation time: 15 minutes
Cooking time: 50 minutes
Total time: 1 hour 5 minutes
Servings: 8

Nutritional Values:

Calories 311, Total Fat 7.6 g, Saturated Fat 2.1 g,
Cholesterol 102 mg, Sodium 250 mg, Total Carbs 37 g,
Fiber 1.4 g, Sugar 4 g, Protein 24.2 g

Ingredients

- 1½ pounds lean ground turkey
- 1 carrot, peeled and chopped
- 1 celery stalk, trimmed and chopped
- 1 cup tomato sauce
- 1 (14-ounce) can stewed, diced tomatoes
- 3 garlic cloves, peeled and minced
- 2 teaspoons coconut sugar
- ½ teaspoon dried basil, crushed
- 1 teaspoon ground cumin
- 1 teaspoon ground coriander
- ½ teaspoon ground turmeric
- 1 (16-ounce) package pasta

How to Prepare

1. Heat a large-sized non-stick saucepan over medium heat and cook turkey for about 8-10 minutes or until browned.
2. Stir in remaining ingredients, except for the pasta, and bring to a gentle boil.
3. Adjust the heat to low and simmer for about 20 minutes.
4. Meanwhile, in a pan of salted boiling water, add pasta and cook for about 8-10 minutes.
5. Drain the pasta well.
6. Add pasta into the pan with the turkey mixture and cook for about 4-5 minutes.
7. Serve hot.

Turkey & Squash Stew

Preparation time: 15 minutes
Cooking time: 45 minutes
Total time: 1 hour
Servings: 8

Nutritional Values:

Calories 247, Total Fat 4.7 g, Saturated Fat 3.1 g,
Cholesterol 70 mg, Sodium 367 mg, Total Carbs 24.3 g,
Fiber 4.5 g, Sugar 8.5 g, Protein 31.6 g

Ingredients

- 2 tablespoons coconut oil
- 2 pounds turkey breast, cubed into 1½-inch size
- 1 onion, peeled and chopped
- 1 (2-inch) piece fresh ginger, peeled and minced
- 5 garlic cloves, peeled and minced
- 1 butternut squash, peeled and cubed
- ¼ teaspoon ground cinnamon
- ¼ teaspoon ground cumin
- 3 cups chicken broth
- 2 pears, cored and chopped
- Salt and ground black pepper, as required
- 1 tablespoon fresh thyme, chopped

How to Prepare

1. In a large-sized-sized heavy-bottomed pan, melt 1 tablespoon of coconut oil over medium-high heat and sear turkey cubes for about 3-4 minutes or until browned completely.
2. With a slotted spoon, transfer the turkey cubes into a bowl.
3. In the same pan, add the onions over medium heat and sauté for about 5 minutes.
4. Add ginger and garlic. Sauté for about 1 minute.
5. Add cooked turkey, squash, cinnamon, cumin, and broth. Cook until boiling.
6. Adjust the heat to low and cook, covered, for about 10 minutes.
7. Stir in pears, salt, and black pepper. Cook, covered, for about 20 minutes.
8. Serve hot with the topping of thyme.

Beef Stew

Preparation time: 20 minutes
Cooking time: 4 hours 10 minutes
Total time: 4½ hours
Servings: 8

Nutritional Values:

Calories 339, Total Fat 12.8 g, Saturated Fat 3.6 g,
Cholesterol 101 mg, Sodium 164 mg, Total Carbs 19.5 g,
Fiber 5.8 g, Sugar 9.2 g, Protein 37 g

Ingredients

- 3 tablespoons olive oil, divided
- 1 large onion, peeled and chopped
- 1 large bell pepper, seeded and chopped
- 4 cups carrots, peeled and chopped
- 1 (14½-ounce) can whole peeled tomatoes, chopped
- 1 sugar pumpkin, cut off the top, seeds and pulp removed
- 4 garlic cloves, peeled and minced
- 1 cup water
- Salt and ground black pepper, as required
- 2 tablespoons beef bouillon granules
- 2 pounds beef stew meat, trimmed and cubed

How to Prepare

1. In a large-sized-sized soup pan, heat 2 tablespoons of oil over medium-high heat and sear beef for about 5 minutes.
2. Stir in vegetables, water, and seasoning. Bring it to a boil.
3. Adjust the heat to low and simmer, covered, for about 2 hours.
4. Preheat your oven to 325ºF.
5. Into the simmering stew, stir in beef bouillon granules and remove from heat.
6. Set the pumpkin in a baking dish.
7. Grease the outside of the pumpkin evenly with remaining oil.
8. Carefully transfer the stew into the hollowed pumpkin.
9. Bake for approximately 2 hours or until pumpkin becomes tender.
10. While serving, scrape some pumpkin meat from inside and serve with the stew.

Beef & Carrot Stew

Preparation time: 15 minutes
Cooking time: 55 minutes
Total time: 1 hour 10 minutes
Servings: 6

Nutritional Values:

Calories 297, Total Fat 10.6 g, Saturated Fat 3.3 g,
Cholesterol 101 mg, Sodium 653 mg, Total Carbs 10.1 g,
Fiber 2.5 g, Sugar 4.7 g, Protein 39.1 g

Ingredients

- 1½ pounds beef stew meat, trimmed and cubed into 1-inch size
- Salt and ground black pepper, as required
- 1 tablespoon olive oil
- 1 cup tomato puree
- 4 cups beef broth
- 2 celery ribs, trimmed and sliced
- 2 cups carrots, peeled and sliced
- 2 garlic cloves, peeled and minced
- ½ tablespoon dried thyme
- 1 teaspoon dried parsley
- 1 teaspoon dried rosemary
- 1 tablespoon paprika
- 1 teaspoon onion powder
- 1 teaspoon garlic powder

How to Prepare

1. In a large-sized bowl, add the beef cubes, salt, and black pepper. Toss to coat well.
2. In a large-sized pan, heat the oil over medium-high heat and cook the beef cubes for about 4-5 minutes or until browned.
3. Add the remaining ingredients and stir to combine.
4. Adjust the heat to high and bring it to a boil.
5. Adjust the heat to low and simmer, covered, for about 40-50 minutes.
6. Stir in the salt and black pepper. Remove from the heat.
7. Serve hot.

Creamy Pork Stew

Preparation time: 15 minutes
Cooking time: 1 hour 35 minutes
Total time: 1 hour 50 minutes
Servings: 8

Nutritional Values:

*Calories 304, Total Fat 12.8 g, Saturated Fat 6.4 g,
Cholesterol 121 mg, Sodium 287 mg, Total Carbs 6.2 g,
Fiber 1.5 g, Sugar 2.9 g, Protein 39.5 g*

Ingredients

- 3 tablespoons unsalted butter
- 2½ pounds boneless pork ribs, cut into ¾-inch cubes
- 1 large yellow onion, peeled and chopped
- 4 garlic cloves, peeled and crushed
- 1½ cups chicken broth
- 2 (10-ounce) cans diced tomatoes
- 2 teaspoons dried oregano
- 1 teaspoon ground cumin
- Salt and ground black pepper, as required
- 2 tablespoons fresh lime juice
- ½ cup sour cream

How to Prepare

1. In a heavy-bottomed soup pan, melt the butter over medium-high heat and cook the pork with garlic and onions for about 5 minutes.
2. Pour in the broth and with a wooden spoon, scrape up the browned bits.
3. Add the tomatoes, oregano, cumin, salt, and back pepper. Stir to combine well.
4. Adjust the heat to medium-low and simmer, covered, for about 1½ hours.
5. Stir in the sour cream and lime juice. Remove from the heat.
6. Serve hot.

Pork & Chiles Stew

Preparation time: 15 minutes
Cooking time: 2¼ hours
Total time: 2½ hours
Servings: 8

Nutritional Values:

Calories 400, Total Fat 19.8 g, Saturated Fat 5.8 g,
Cholesterol 122 mg, Sodium 308 mg, Total Carbs 9.8 g,
Fiber 3.1 g, Sugar 5.6 g, Protein 44.4 g

Ingredients

- 3 tablespoons olive oil
- 2½ pounds pork stew meat, cut into ¾-inch cubes
- 1 large white onion, peeled and chopped
- 2 celery stalks, trimmed and chopped
- 3 garlic cloves, peeled and crushed
- 2 cups chicken broth
- 1 (28-ounce) cans diced tomatoes
- 1 cup canned roasted poblano chiles
- 2 teaspoons dried thyme
- Salt, as required
- 2 tablespoons fresh lemon juice
- ¼ cup fresh cilantro, chopped

How to Prepare

1. IIn a large-sized Dutch oven, heat olive oil over medium-high heat and cook the pork cubes for about 4-5 minutes.
2. With a slotted spoon, transfer the pork cubes into a bowl.
3. In the pan, add in the onions, celery, and garlic. Cook for about 5 minutes.
4. Add the cooked pork meat, broth, tomatoes, poblano chiles, thyme, and salt. Bring it to a boil.
5. Adjust the heat to medium-low and simmer, covered, for about 2 hours.
6. Stir in the lemon juice and serve hot with the garnishing of cilantro.

Salmon & Shrimp Stew

Preparation time: 15 minutes
Cooking time: 25 minutes
Total time: 40 minutes
Servings: 6

Nutritional Values:

Calories 286, Total Fat 11.8 g, Saturated Fat 5.3 g,
Cholesterol 193 mg, Sodium 735 mg, Total Carbs 8.3 g,
Fiber 2 g, Sugar 4.2 g, Protein 36.6 g

Ingredients

- 2 tablespoons coconut oil
- ½ cup onion, peeled and chopped finely
- 2 garlic cloves, peeled and minced
- 1 Serrano pepper, chopped
- 1 teaspoon smoked paprika
- 1 teaspoon ground cumin
- ½ teaspoon ground turmeric
- 4 cups fresh tomatoes, chopped
- 4 cups chicken broth
- 1 pound salmon fillets, cubed
- 1 pound shrimp, peeled and deveined
- 2 tablespoons fresh lime juice
- Salt and ground black pepper, as required
- 3 tablespoons fresh parsley, chopped

How to Prepare

1. In a large-sized soup pan, melt coconut oil over medium-high heat and sauté the onions for about 5-6 minutes.
2. Add the garlic, Serrano pepper, and paprika. Sauté for about 1 minute.
3. Add the tomatoes and broth. Bring it to a boil.
4. Adjust the heat to medium and simmer for about 5 minutes.
5. Add the salmon and simmer for about 3-4 minutes.
6. Stir in the shrimp and cook for about 4-5 minutes.
7. Stir in lemon juice, salt, and black pepper. Serve hot with the garnishing of parsley.

Seafood Stew

Preparation time: 20 minutes
Cooking time: 25 minutes
Total time: 45 minutes
Servings: 6

Nutritional Values:

Calories 242, Total Fat 8.3 g, Saturated Fat 1.6 g,
Cholesterol 159 mg, Sodium 711 mg, Total Carbs 10.2 g,
Fiber 2 g, Sugar 4.3 g, Protein 31.4 g

Ingredients

- 2 tablespoons olive oil
- ½ cup white onion, peeled and chopped finely
- 2 garlic cloves, peeled and minced
- 1 fresh red chili, chopped finely
- 1 teaspoon smoked paprika
- 4 cups fresh tomatoes, chopped
- 4½ cups chicken broth
- ½ pound tilapia fillets, cubed
- ½ pound shrimp, peeled and deveined
- ¼ pound fresh squid, cleaned and cut into rings
- ¼ pound fresh bay scallops, rinsed and pat dried
- ½ pound mussels, cleaned and debearded
- 2 tablespoons fresh lemon juice
- ½ cup fresh parsley, chopped finely
- Salt and ground black pepper, as required

How to Prepare

1. In a large-sized soup pan, heat oil over medium-high heat and sauté onions for about 5-6 minutes.
2. Add the garlic, red chili, and paprika. Sauté for about 1 minute.
3. Add the tomatoes and broth. Bring it to a boil.
4. Adjust the heat to medium and cook for about 5 minutes.
5. Stir in the tilapia and simmer for about 2-3 minutes.
6. Stir in the remaining seafood and cook for about 4-5 minutes.
7. Stir in the lemon juice, parsley, salt, and black pepper. Serve hot.

Mushroom Stew

Preparation time: 15 minutes
Cooking time: 20 minutes
Total time: 35 minutes
Servings: 4

Nutritional Values:

Calories 167, Total Fat 14.7 g, Saturated Fat 7.4 g,
Cholesterol 0 mg, Sodium 1711 mg, Total Carbs 7.8 g,
Fiber 2.3 g, Sugar 3.9 g, Protein 4.9 g

Ingredients

- 2 tablespoons olive oil
- 1 small yellow onion, peeled and chopped
- 2 garlic cloves, peeled and minced
- ½ pound fresh button mushrooms, cleaned and sliced
- ¼ pound fresh shiitake mushrooms, cleaned and sliced
- ¼ pound fresh Portobello mushrooms, cleaned and sliced
- Salt and ground black pepper, as required
- ½ cup unsweetened coconut milk
- ¼ cup vegetable broth
- 2 tablespoons fresh lemon juice
- 1 tablespoon fresh parsley, chopped

How to Prepare

1. In a large-sized skillet, heat the oil over medium heat and sauté the onions and garlic for about 5 minutes.
2. Stir in the mushrooms, salt, and black pepper. Cook for about 5-7 minutes or until all the liquid is absorbed.
3. Stir in the coconut milk and broth. Bring to a gentle boil.
4. Simmer for about 5 minutes or until the desired doneness.
5. Stir in lemon juice and parsley. Remove from the heat.
6. Serve hot.

Veggie Stew

Preparation time: 15 minutes
Cooking time: 40 minutes
Total time: 55 minutes
Servings: 8

Nutritional Values:

Calories 175, Total Fat 4.5 g, Saturated Fat 3.2 g,
Cholesterol 0 mg, Sodium429 mg, Total Carbs 29 g, Fiber
5.5 g, Sugar 5.2 g, Protein 5.8

Ingredients

- 2 tablespoons coconut oil
- 1 large sweet onion, peeled and chopped
- 1 medium parsnip, peeled and chopped
- 3 tablespoons tomato paste
- 4 garlic cloves, peeled and minced
- 1 teaspoon ground cumin
- ½ teaspoon ground cinnamon
- ½ teaspoon ground ginger
- ¼ teaspoon cayenne pepper
- 2 medium carrots, peeled and chopped
- 2 medium purple potatoes, peeled and chopped
- 2 medium sweet potatoes, peeled and chopped
- 4 cups vegetable broth
- 2 tablespoons fresh lemon juice
- 1 cup frozen green peas
- Salt and ground black pepper, as required
- ¼ cup fresh cilantro leaves, chopped

How to Prepare

1. In a large-sized-sized Dutch oven, melt the coconut oil over medium-high heat and sauté the onions for about 5 minutes.
2. Add the parsnip and sauté for about 3 minutes.
3. Stir in tomato paste, garlic, and spices. Sauté for about 2 minutes.
4. Add the carrots, potatoes, and sweet potatoes. Stir to combine.
5. Add the broth and bring it to a boil.
6. Adjust the heat to medium-low and simmer for about 20 minutes.
7. Stir in the lemon juice and green peas. Simmer for about 4-5 minutes.
8. Stir in the salt and black pepper. Serve hot with the garnishing of cilantro.

Tofu & Vegetable Stew

Preparation time: 15 minutes
Cooking time: 30 minutes
Total time: 45 minutes
Servings: 6

Nutritional Values:

*Calories 126, Total Fat 5.3 g, Saturated Fat 0.6 g,
Cholesterol 0 mg, Sodium 483 mg, Total Carbs 11.4 g,
Fiber 2.9 g, Sugar 5.6 g, Protein 11.8 g*

Ingredients

- 2 tablespoons garlic, peeled
- 1 jalapeño pepper, seeded and chopped
- 1 (16-ounce) jar roasted red peppers, rinsed, drained, and chopped
- 2 cups vegetable broth
- 2 cups water
- 1 medium red bell pepper, seeded and thinly sliced
- 1 small zucchini, sliced
- 1 (16-ounce) package extra-firm tofu, drained and cubed
- 1 (10-ounce) package frozen spinach, thawed

How to Prepare

1. In a food processor, place the garlic, jalapeño pepper, and roasted red peppers and pulse until smooth.
2. In a large-sized pan, add the peppers puree, broth, and water over medium-high heat and bring it to a boil
3. Add the bell pepper, zucchini, and tofu. Stir to combine.
4. Adjust the heat to medium and cook for about 5 minutes.
5. Stir in the spinach and cook for about 5 minutes.
6. Serve hot.

Black Beans Stew

Preparation time: 10 minutes
Cooking time: 30 minutes
Total time: 40 minutes
Servings: 4

Nutritional Values:

*Calories 334, Total Fat 5.1 g, Saturated Fat 0.9 g,
Cholesterol 0 mg, Sodium 153 mg, Total Carbs 55.7 g,
Fiber 19.2 g, Sugar 4.9 g, Protein 19.3 g*

Ingredients

- 1 tablespoon olive oil
- 2 small onions, peeled and chopped
- 1 small carrot, peeled and chopped
- 5 garlic cloves, peeled and chopped finely
- 1 teaspoon of dried oregano
- 1 teaspoon ground cumin
- ½ teaspoon ground ginger
- Salt and ground black pepper, as required
- 1 (14-ounce) can diced tomatoes
- 2 (13½-ounce) cans black beans, rinsed and drained
- ½ cup vegetable broth

How to Prepare

1. Heat the olive oil in a pan over medium heat and cook the onions and carrot for about 5-7 minutes, stirring frequently.
2. Add garlic, oregano, spices, salt, and black pepper. Cook for about 1 minute.
3. Add the tomatoes and cook for about 1-2 minutes.
4. Add in the beans and broth. Bring it to a boil.
5. Adjust the heat to medium-low and simmer, covered, for about 15 minutes.
6. Serve hot.

Chickpeas & Spinach Stew

Preparation time: 15 minutes
Cooking time: 35 minutes
Total time: 50 minutes
Servings: 4

Nutritional Values:

Calories 250, Total Fat 5.9 g, Saturated Fat 0.9 g,
Cholesterol 0 mg, Sodium 711 mg, Total Carbs 40.5 g,
Fiber 8.8 g, Sugar 6.8 g, Protein 10.5 g

Ingredients

- 1 tablespoon olive oil
- 1 medium onion, peeled and chopped
- 2 cups carrots, peeled and chopped
- 2 garlic cloves, peeled and minced
- 1 teaspoon red pepper flakes
- 2 large tomatoes, peeled, seeded and chopped finely
- 2 cups vegetable broth
- 2 cups cooked chickpeas
- 2 cups fresh spinach, chopped
- 1 tablespoon fresh lemon juice
- Salt and ground black pepper, as required

How to Prepare

1. In a large-sized pan, heat oil over medium heat and sauté the onions and carrots for about 6 minutes.
2. Stir in the garlic and red pepper flakes. Sauté for about 1 minute.
3. Add the tomatoes and cook for about 2-3 minutes.
4. Add the broth and bring it to a boil.
5. Adjust the heat to low and simmer for about 10 minutes.
6. Stir in the chickpeas and simmer for about 5 minutes.
7. Stir in the spinach and simmer for 3-4 minutes more.
8. Stir in the lemon juice and seasoning. Remove from the heat.
9. Serve hot.

Chickpeas & Squash Stew

Preparation time: 15 minutes
Cooking time: 1¼ hours
Total time: 1½ hours
Servings: 4

Nutritional Values:

*Calories 223, Total Fat 2.6 g, Saturated Fat 0.4 g,
Cholesterol 0 mg, Sodium 325 mg, Total Carbs 46.1 g,
Fiber 9.8 g, Sugar 9 g, Protein 8 g*

Ingredients

- 2 tablespoons avocado oil
- 1 large white onion, peeled and chopped
- 4 garlic cloves, peeled and minced
- ½ tablespoon cayenne powder
- 4 large plum tomatoes, seeded and chopped finely
- 1 pound butternut squash, peeled, seeded, and chopped
- 2 cups water
- 1½ cups cooked chickpeas
- 2 tablespoons fresh lime juice
- Salt and ground black pepper, as required
- 2 tablespoons fresh parsley, chopped

How to Prepare

1. In a soup pan, heat the avocado oil over medium heat and sauté the onions for about 4-6 minutes.
2. Add the garlic and cayenne powder. Sauté for about 1 minute.
3. Add the tomatoes and cook for about 2-3 minutes.
4. Add the squash and water. Bring it to a boil.
5. Adjust the heat to low and simmer, covered, for about 50 minutes.
6. Add the chickpeas and cook for about 10 minutes.
7. Stir in lime juice, salt, and black pepper. Remove from heat.
8. Serve hot with the garnishing of parsley.

Lentil & Barley Stew

Preparation time: 20 minutes
Cooking time: 50 minutes
Total time: 1 hour 10 minutes
Servings: 8

Nutritional Values:

*Calories 266, Total Fat 5.6 g, Saturated Fat 0.9 g,
Cholesterol 0 mg, Sodium 523 mg, Total Carbs 42 g,
Fiber 14 g, Sugar 6.5 g, Protein 13.8 g*

Ingredients

- 2 tablespoons olive oil
- 2 carrots, peeled and chopped
- 2 large red onions, peeled and chopped
- 2 celery stalks, trimmed and chopped
- 2 garlic cloves, peeled and minced
- 1 teaspoon ground coriander
- 2 teaspoons ground cumin
- 1 teaspoon cayenne pepper
- 1 cup barley
- 1 cup red lentils
- 5 cups tomatoes, chopped finely
- 5-6 cups vegetable broth
- Salt and ground black pepper, as required

How to Prepare

1. In a large-sized pan, heat the oil over medium heat and sauté the carrots, onions, and celery for about 5 minutes.
2. Add the garlic and spices. Sauté for about 1 minute.
3. Add the barley, lentils, tomatoes, and broth. Bring to a rolling boil.
4. Adjust the heat to low and simmer, covered, for about 40 minutes.
5. Stir in the spinach, salt, and black pepper. Simmer for about 3-4 minutes.
6. Serve hot.

123

This page is for your notes

This page is for your notes

This page is for your notes

This page is for your notes

This page is for your notes

Bowls Recipes

Chicken & Apple Bowl

Preparation time: 15 minutes
Cooking time: 16 minutes
Total time: 31 minutes
Servings: 8

Nutritional Values:

Calories 436, Total Fat 25.7 g, Saturated Fat 3 g,
Cholesterol 66 mg, Sodium 102 mg, Total Carbs 25.9 g,
Fiber 5.9 g, Sugar 17.2 g, Protein 28.8 g

Ingredients

Chicken
- 2 pounds boneless, skinless chicken breasts
- ½ cup olive oil
- ¼ cup fresh lemon juice
- 2 tablespoons sugar
- 1 garlic clove, peeled and minced
- Salt and ground black pepper, as required

Bowl
- 4 large apples, cored and sliced
- 2 cups dried cranberries
- 1 cup pecans
- 12 cups lettuce, torn

How to Prepare

1. For marinade: in a large-sized bowl, add the oil, lemon juice, sugar, garlic, salt, and black pepper. Beat until well combined.
2. In a large-sized, resealable plastic bag, place chicken and ¾ cup of marinade.
3. Seal the bag and shake to coat well.
4. Refrigerate overnight.
5. Cover the bowl of remaining marinade and refrigerate before serving.
6. Preheat the grill to medium heat.
7. Grease the grill grate.
8. Remove the chicken from bag and discard the marinade.
9. Place the chicken onto grill grate and grill, covered, for about 5-8 minutes per side.
10. Remove the chicken from the grill and cut into strips.
11. Divide the chicken strips, apple slices, cranberries, pecans, and lettuce into serving bowls.
12. Drizzle with reserved marinade and serve.

Chicken & Veggie Bowl

Preparation time: 15 minutes
Cooking time: 16 minutes
Total time: 31 minutes
Servings: 6

Nutritional Values:

*Calories 300, Total Fat 16.7 g, Saturated Fat 3.9 g,
Cholesterol 83 mg, Sodium 155 mg, Total Carbs 11.8 g,
Fiber 1.8 g, Sugar 4.3 g, Protein 26.3 g*

Ingredients

Chicken
- 4 (6-ounce) boneless, skinless chicken breast halves
- Salt and ground black pepper, as required
- 2 tablespoons butter

Dressing
- 4 tablespoon olive oil
- 3 tablespoons balsamic vinegar
- 1 tablespoon fresh lemon juice
- Salt and ground black pepper, as required

Bowl
- 3 cucumbers, sliced
- 3 tomatoes, sliced
- 1 cup croutons
- 6 cups fresh baby greens

How to Prepare

1. Season each chicken breast half with salt and black pepper evenly.
2. Place chicken over a rack set in a rimmed baking sheet.
3. Refrigerate for at least 30 minutes.
4. Remove the chicken breast halves from the refrigerator and pat dry with paper towels.
5. Melt the butter in a 12-inch sauté pan over medium-low heat.
6. Place the chicken breast halves, smooth side down, and cook for about 9-10 minutes, without moving.
7. Flip the chicken breasts and cook for about 6 minutes or until cooked through.
8. Remove the sauté pan from heat and let the chicken stand in the pan for about 3 minutes.
9. Meanwhile, for dressing: in a bowl, add all ingredients and whisk until well combined.
10. Cut each chicken breast into slices.
11. Divide the chicken slices, cucumbers, tomatoes, croutons, and baby greens into serving bowls.
12. Drizzle with dressing and serve.

Chicken & Quinoa Bowl

Preparation time: 15 minutes
Cooking time: 15 minutes
Total time: 30 minutes
Servings: 4

Nutritional Values:

Calories 434, Total Fat 20.6 g, Saturated Fat 3.1 g,
Cholesterol 66 mg, Sodium 275 mg, Total Carbs 30.5 g,
Fiber 7.2 g, Sugar 3.1 g, Protein 33.5 g

Ingredients

Chicken
- 4 (4-ounce) boneless, skinless chicken breasts
- Salt and ground black pepper, as required
- 2 tablespoons olive oil
- ¾ cup chicken broth

Bowl
- 1 cup cooked quinoa
- 1 large avocado, peeled, pitted and slices
- 1 large tomato, chopped
- 4 cups lettuce, torn
- 1 lime, cut into wedges
- 2 tablespoons fresh cilantro, chopped

How to Prepare

1. Season the chicken breasts with salt and black pepper evenly.
2. In a large-sized skillet, heat the oil over medium heat and cook the chicken breasts for about 5 minutes.
3. Flip the chicken breast and top with the broth.
4. Cook, covered, for about 7-10 minutes or until cooked through.
5. With a slotted spoon, transfer the chicken breast into a bowl.
6. Cut the chicken breasts into desired-sized slices.
7. Divide the chicken slices, quinoa, avocado, tomato, and lettuce into serving bowls.
8. Serve with the topping of lime wedges and cilantro.

Steak Bowl

Preparation time: 15 minutes
Cooking time: 12 minutes
Total time: 27 minutes
Servings: 3

Nutritional Values:

Calories 482, Total Fat 35.2 g, Saturated Fat 11.6 g,
Cholesterol 75 mg, Sodium 625 mg, Total Carbs 20.4 g,
Fiber 3.3 g, Sugar 12.5 g, Protein 23.4 g

Ingredients

Steak
- 1 tablespoon low-sodium soy sauce
- 1 teaspoon Montreal steak seasoning
- 1 (12-ounce) rib-eye steak

Dressing
- 2 tablespoons olive oil
- 2 tablespoons fresh lemon juice
- 1 tablespoon sugar
- ¼ teaspoon garlic powder
- 1/8 teaspoon red pepper flakes, crushed
- Salt and ground black pepper, as required

Bowl
- 2 English cucumbers, cubed
- 2 large tomatoes, chopped
- ¼ cup red onion, peeled and sliced
- 5 cups romaine lettuce leaves, torn
- 1 fresh red chili, sliced
- 1 tablespoon fresh cilantro leaves

How to Prepare

1. For steak: in a large-sized bowl, mix together the soy sauce and steak seasoning.
2. Add the steak and coat with the seasoning mixture evenly.
3. Cover the bowl of steak mixture and refrigerate to marinate for at least 1 hour.
4. Preheat the grill to medium-high heat.
5. Grease the grill grate.
6. Place the steak onto the grill and cook for about 6 minutes per side.
7. Remove from the grill and place the steak onto a cutting board.
8. Set aside for about 10 minutes before slicing.
9. Cut the beef steak diagonally into slices across the grain.
10. In a small-sized bowl, add all dressing ingredients and beat until well combined.
11. Divide the steak slices, cucumber, tomato, and lettuce into serving bowls.
12. Drizzle with dressing and serve with the topping of red chili and cilantro.

Smoked Salmon Bowl

Preparation time: 15 minutes
Total time: 15 minutes
Servings: 2

Nutritional Values:

*Calories 334, Total Fat 23.2 g, Saturated Fat 6 g,
Cholesterol 43 mg, Sodium 1140 mg, Total Carbs 7.2 g,
Fiber 2.2 g, Sugar 4.6 g, Protein 25.2 g*

Ingredients

Dressin
- 2 tablespoons olive oil
- 1 tablespoon fresh lemon juice
- 1 teaspoon Dijon mustard
- Salt and ground black pepper, as required

Bowl
- ½ pound smoked salmon, cut into bite-sized pieces
- 4 cups fresh baby greens
- 1 cup tomatoes, sliced
- ¼ cup red onion, peeled and sliced
- ¼ cup feta cheese, cubed

How to Prepare

1. In a small-sized bowl, add all dressing ingredients and beat until well combined.
2. Divide the smoked salmon, tomato, onion, greens, and feta into serving bowls.
3. Drizzle with dressing and serve.

Tuna Bowl

Preparation time: 15 minutes
Total time: 15 minutes
Servings: 6

Nutritional Values:

*Calories 271, Total Fat 12.7 g, Saturated Fat 2 g,
Cholesterol 57 mg, Sodium 383 mg, Total Carbs 10.4 g,
Fiber 3.4 g, Sugar 4.4 g, Protein 33.2 g*

Ingredients

Dressing
- 3 tablespoons olive oil
- 2 tablespoons fresh lime juice
- 2 tablespoons mustard
- Salt and ground black pepper, as required

Bowl
- 2 (6-ounce) cans olive oil-packed tuna, drained and flaked
- 2 (6-ounce) cans water-packed tuna, drained and flaked
- 2 large bell peppers (green and yellow), seeded and chopped
- 1½ cups cherry tomatoes, halved
- 1 cup onion, peeled and chopped
- 1 cup black olives, pitted and sliced
- 6 cups fresh baby spinach

How to Prepare

1. In a small-sized bowl, add all dressing ingredients and beat until well combined.
2. Divide the smoked salmon, tomato, onion, greens, and feta into serving bowls.
3. Drizzle with dressing and serve.

Shrimp Bowl

Preparation time: 15 minutes
Cooking time: 3 minutes
Total time: 18 minutes
Servings: 4

Nutritional Values:

Calories 162, Total Fat 6.3 g, Saturated Fat 1.2 g,
Cholesterol 159 mg, Sodium 222 mg, Total Carbs 8.2 g,
Fiber 1.6 g, Sugar 3.8 g, Protein 19 g

Ingredients

Shrimp
- 1 pound shrimp, peeled and deveined
- 1 lemon, quartered

Dressin
- 2 tablespoons olive oil
- 2 teaspoons fresh lemon juice
- Salt and ground black pepper, as required

Bowl
- 2 large tomatoes, sliced
- 2 large cucumbers, sliced
- 6 cups fresh baby arugula

How to Prepare

1. In a pan of lightly salted boiling water, add the quartered lemon.
2. Add the shrimp and cook for about 2-3 minutes or until pink and opaque.
3. With a slotted spoon, transfer the shrimp into a bowl of ice water to stop the cooking process.
4. Drain the shrimp completely and then pat dry with paper towels.
5. In a small-sized bowl, add the oil, lemon juice, salt, and black pepper, and beat until well combined.
6. Divide the shrimp, tomato, cucumber, and arugula into serving bowls.
7. Drizzle with oil mixture and serve.

Green Veggies & Avocado Bowl

Preparation time: 15 minutes
Cooking time: 2 minutes
Total time: 17 minutes
Servings: 4

Nutritional Values:

Calories 282, Total Fat 21.3 g, Saturated Fat 3.8 g,
Cholesterol 0 mg, Sodium 146 mg, Total Carbs 21.5 g,
Fiber 8.7 g, Sugar 6.9 g, Protein 7.1 g

Ingredients

Dressing
- 3 tablespoons olive oil
- 3 tablespoons fresh lemon juice
- 1 tablespoon Dijon mustard
- 1 teaspoon fresh lemon zest, grated
- Salt and ground black pepper, as required

Bowl
- 1½ cups broccoli florets
- 2 small zucchinis, cut into ribbons
- 2 cucumbers, cut into ribbons
- 1 cup frozen green peas, thawed
- 1 large avocado, peeled, pitted, and sliced
- 6 cups fresh baby spinach

How to Prepare

1. For the bowl: in a saucepan of lightly salted boiling water, add the broccoli florets and cook for about 1-2 minutes.
2. Drain the broccoli and immediately place into a bowl of iced water for 5 minutes.
3. Again, drain the broccoli and pat dry with a clean tea towel.
4. For dressing: in a small-sized bowl, add all the ingredients and beat until well combined.
5. Divide the cooked broccoli, zucchini, cucumbers, green peas, avocado, and spinach into serving bowls.
6. Drizzle with dressing and serve.

Veggie Bowl

Preparation time: 15 minutes
Total time: 15 minutes
Servings: 6

Nutritional Values:

*Calories 128, Total Fat 8.9 g, Saturated Fat 1.3 g,
Cholesterol 0 mg, Sodium 41 mg, Total Carbs 12.7 g,
Fiber 2.8 g, Sugar 6.4 g, Protein 2.5 g*

Ingredients

Dressin
- ¼ cup olive oil
- 2 tablespoons fresh lemon juice
- 1 small garlic clove, peeled and minced finely
- ½ teaspoon dried oregano, crushed
- ½ teaspoon dried basil, crushed
- Salt and ground black pepper, as required

Bowl
- 3 large cucumbers, peeled and chopped
- 3 cups cherry tomatoes, halved
- 1 cup onion, peeled and sliced
- 4 cups fresh salad greens
- 4 cups lettuce, torn

How to Prepare

1. For dressing: in a small-sized bowl, add all the ingredients and beat until well combined.
2. Divide the cucumbers, tomatoes, onion, salad greens, and lettuce into serving bowls.
3. Drizzle with dressing and serve.

Mixed Berries Salad Bowl

Preparation time: 10 minutes
Total time: 10 minutes
Servings: 2

Nutritional Values:

Calories 364, Total Fat 30.4 g, Saturated Fat 6.1 g,
Cholesterol 17 mg, Sodium 327 mg, Total Carbs 21.5 g,
Fiber 5.6 g, Sugar 13.4 g, Protein 6.8 g

Ingredients

Dressing
- 2 tablespoons olive oil
- 2 tablespoons fresh lemon juice
- 1 teaspoon honey
- 1/8 teaspoon garlic powder
- Salt, as required

Bowl
- ¾ cup fresh strawberries, hulled and sliced
- ¾ cup fresh blueberries
- ¼ cup onion, peeled and sliced
- ¼ cup pecans
- ¼ cup feta cheese, crumbled
- 3 cups fresh baby spinach

How to Prepare

1. For dressing: In a small-sized bowl, add all the ingredients and beat until well combined.
2. Divide the berries, onion, pecans, feta, and spinach into serving bowls.
3. Drizzle with the dressing and serve.

Conclusion

Did you know that soup has been around for centuries? It's no wonder this delicious and nutritious dish is still popular today. Whether you're looking to warm up on a cold day or simply satisfy your hunger, there's a soup out there for everyone. So next time you're in the mood for something comforting, give soup a try!

This page is for your notes

This page is for your notes

This page is for your notes

Made in United States
Orlando, FL
13 August 2023

36048902R00078